Rock Climbing
SHELF ROAD

by
Ma

A FALCON GUIDE®

Falcon® Publishing is continually expanding its list of recreational guidebooks. All books include detailed descriptions, accurate maps, and all the information necessary for enjoyable trips. You can order extra copies of this book and get information and prices for other Falcon guidebooks by writing Falcon, P.O. Box 1718, Helena, MT 59624 or calling toll-free 1-800-582-2665. Also, please ask for a free copy of our current catalog. Visit our website at www.FalconOutdoors.com or contact us by e-mail at falcon.falcon.com.

© 1999 by Mark Van Horn
Printed in the United States of America.

1 2 3 4 5 6 7 8 9 0 PU 04 03 02 01 00 99

Falcon and FalconGuide are registered trademarks of Falcon® Publishing, Inc.

Black and white photos by Mark Van Horn unless otherwise noted.

Library of Congress Cataloging-in-Publication Data

Van Horn, Mark.
    Rock climbing Colorado's Shelf Road / by Mark Van Horn.
        p. cm.—(A FalconGuide)
    Rev. ed. of: Shelf Road rock guide. 1990.
    "Chockstone."
    Includes indexes.
    ISBN 1-56044-752-4 (pbk.)
        1. Rock climbing—Colorado—Canon City Region—Guidebooks.
    2. Canon City Region (Colo.)—Guidebooks. I. Van Horn, Mark.
    Shelf Road rock guide. II. Title. III. Series: Falcon guide.
    GV199.42.C62C368 1999
    796.52'23'0978853—dc21   99-17801
                                                                  CIP

CAUTION

Outdoor recreational activities are by their very nature potentially hazardous. All participants in such activities must assume the responsibility for their own actions and safety. The information contained in this guidebook cannot replace sound judgment and good decision-making skills, which help reduce risk exposure, nor does the scope of this book allow for disclosure of all the potential hazards and risks involved in such activities.

Learn as much as possible about the outdoor recreational activities in which you participate, prepare for the unexpected, and be cautious. The reward will be a safer and more enjoyable experience.

 Text pages printed on recycled paper.

WARNING:
CLIMBING IS A SPORT WHERE
YOU MAY BE SERIOUSLY INJURED OR DIE.
READ THIS BEFORE YOU USE THIS BOOK.

This guidebook is a compilation of unverified information gathered from many different climbers. The author cannot assure the accuracy of any of the information in this book, including the topos and route descriptions, the difficulty ratings, and the protection ratings. These may be incorrect or misleading and it is impossible for any one author to climb all the routes to confirm the information about each route. Also, ratings of climbing difficulty and danger are always subjective and depend on the physical characteristics (for example, height), experience, technical ability, confidence and physical fitness of the climber who supplied the rating. Additionally, climbers who achieve first ascents sometimes underrate the difficulty or danger of the climbing route out of fear of being ridiculed if a climb is later down-rated by subsequent ascents. Therefore, be warned that you must exercise your own judgment on where a climbing route goes, its difficulty and your ability to safely protect yourself from the risks of rock climbing. Examples of some of these risks are: falling due to technical difficulty or due to natural hazards such as holds breaking, falling rock, climbing equipment dropped by other climbers, hazards of weather and lightning, your own equipment failure, and failure or absence of fixed protection.

You should not depend on any information gleaned from this book for your personal safety; your safety depends on your own good judgment, based on experience and a realistic assessment of your climbing ability. If you have any doubt as to your ability to safely climb a route described in this book, do not attempt it.

The following are some ways to make your use of this book safer:

1. **CONSULTATION**: You should consult with other climbers about the difficulty and danger of a particular climb prior to attempting it. Most local climbers are glad to give advice on routes in their area and we suggest that you contact locals to confirm ratings and safety of particular routes and to obtain first-hand information about a route chosen from this book.

2. **INSTRUCTION**: Most climbing areas have local climbing instructors and guides available. We recommend that you engage an instructor or guide to learn safety techniques and to become familiar with the routes and hazards of the areas described in this book. Even after you are proficient in climbing safely, occasional use of a guide is a safe way to raise your climbing standard and learn advanced techniques.

3. **FIXED PROTECTION**: Many of the routes in this book use bolts and pitons which are permanently placed in the rock. Because of variations in the manner of placement, weathering, metal fatigue, the quality of the metal used, and many other factors, these fixed protection pieces should always be considered suspect and should always be backed up by equipment that you place yourself. Never depend for your safety on a single piece of fixed protection because you never can tell whether it will hold weight, and in some cases, fixed protection may have been removed or is now absent.

Be aware of the following specific potential hazards which could arise in using this book:

1. **MISDESCRIPTIONS OF ROUTES**: If you climb a route and you have a doubt as to where the route may go, you should not go on unless you are sure that you can go that way safely. Route descriptions and topos in this book may be inaccurate or misleading.

2. **INCORRECT DIFFICULTY RATING**: A route may, in fact, be more difficult than the rating indicates. Do not be lulled into a false sense of security by the difficulty rating.

3. **INCORRECT PROTECTION RATING**: If you climb a route and you are unable to arrange adequate protection from the risk of falling through the use of fixed pitons or bolts and by placing your own protection devices, do not assume that there is adequate protection available higher just because the route protection rating indicates the route is not an "X" or an "R" rating. Every route is potentially an "X" (a fall may be deadly), due to the inherent hazards of climbing – including, for example, failure or absence of fixed protection, your own equipment's failure, or improper use of climbing equipment.

THERE ARE NO WARRANTIES, WHETHER EXPRESS OR IMPLIED, THAT THIS GUIDEBOOK IS ACCURATE OR THAT THE INFORMATION CONTAINED IN IT IS RELIABLE. THERE ARE NO WARRANTIES OF FITNESS FOR A PARTICULAR PURPOSE OR THAT THIS GUIDE IS MERCHANTABLE. YOUR USE OF THIS BOOK INDICATES YOUR ASSUMPTION OF THE RISK THAT IT MAY CONTAIN ERRORS AND IS AN ACKNOWLEDGMENT OF YOUR OWN SOLE RESPONSIBILITY FOR YOUR CLIMBING SAFETY.

CONTENTS

PREFACE

This is the second comprehensive guidebook to rock climbing in the Shelf Road Recreation Area. Since climbing activity began on Bureau of Land Management (BLM) property, over 400 routes have been established. It is the purpose of this guidebook to provide information on all the rock climbs within the BLM's public lands. Climbing routes on non-public lands (i.e. Private and State Trust land) are omitted from this guidebook. Routes are described using a modified "topo" method. While utilizing standard topo representations, the drawings are more graphic, reflecting a more artistic approach. These modified topos are used due to the short nature of Shelf Road climbs; hopefully these topos will make it easier for the users of this book to identify the climbs. Also accompanying the topos are U.S. and French grading system ratings and route quality ratings (0-3 stars). Brief written descriptions (i.e. adjectives) are included with most routes to indicate the type or style of climbing encountered.

At press time in the spring of 1999, the Access Fund and the BLM teamed up to purchase private land that had previously been closed to climbing. This edition was temporarily delayed to allow the inclusion of the recently opened cliffs. Please refer to the Access Fund Statement at the back of the book for more information.

Attention to detail is important to the author; however, mistakes are unavoidable and situations are always changing. Any information, recommendations or corrections are helpful and welcomed by the author. Please send updates to:

Rock Climbing Shelf Road
Falcon Publishing Co., Inc.
P.O. Box 1718
Helena Montana 59624

ACKNOWLEDGMENTS

The author would like to express his thanks to all the people who have helped make this book possible, as well as those who have invested their time and energy towards the improvement of the Shelf Road area. These people and organizations include: Rosalie Van Horn; Darryl Roth; Dan Durland; Ric Geiman; Erick Christianson; Kieron Hardy; Dan Monroe; Mike Johnson; Earl Wiggins; Wayne Meyer; Mark Hesse (Rocky Mountain Field Institute); Rick Thompson (Access Fund); Diana Kossnar (BLM); Leah Quesenberry (BLM); QUAD-DUSTERS (Colorado Springs), and the Rocky Mountain Backcountry Horsemen. It is likely this book would never have been completed without the generous efforts and support of these people. I would also, once again, like to thank George Meyers of Chockstone Press for his patience, expertise and assistance. Lastly, I thank John Burbidge and Falcon Publishing for producing this edition.

FOREWORD (TO THE SECOND EDITION)
BY RIC GEIMAN

How do you characterize a truly great climbing area? What factors need to be considered? Since climbers are such a diverse group, there is no definitive answer. There are, however, some factors that, when combined, will put the quality of one area above others. Shelf Road without question possesses all the components of a superb area.

First, a great rock climbing area must have great rock. Shelf's limestone, although not consistent, has extensive areas where the rock is incredible. The Gymnasium, The Bank, The Dark Side, The Gallery, and Sand Gulch all have sections with perfect limestone. If you have climbed on this medium, you know its character: pockets, edges, interesting movement, solid and steep. The best!!!

Quality also can be found in an area's environment. Shelf Road's high desert climate is excellent. It's extremely rare to have your day of climbing shut down by the weather. The orientation of the canyons at Shelf Road allows one to quickly head for sunshine if it's cold and seek shade if it's hot. The views from all the crags—The Gymnasium in particular—are breathtaking. Helena Canyon to the east and the snow-covered Sangre de Cristo Mountains to the south provides inspiring scenery.

Shelf Road possesses all the attributes of a "mature" climbing area. The Bureau of Land Management, American Mountain Foundation, and hundreds of volunteers have built an extensive trail system, roads have been improved, restroom facilities installed, and two campgrounds have been added. As for the routes, Shelf was one of Colorado's first sport climbing areas. Establishment of routes began in earnest in the late 1980s and continues today, though at a less frenzied pace. The total number of climbs by now must be over one thousand, and there are close to 100 with a three-star quality rating. The routes are spread out enough to eliminate the crowding problems that plague many climbing areas, yet the approaches are short. Finding these routes is now easier than ever with the publication of this latest edition of the *Shelf Road Rock Guide*, now called *Rock Climbing Shelf Road*.

FOREWORD (TO THE FIRST EDITION)
BY DARRYL ROTH

Wolfgang Güllich, in an 1987 interview published by *Climbing* magazine, observed: "Limestone has a wider variety of climbing than any other type of rock. Finger cracks, roofs, face climbs through bulges and steep slabs....one must analyze a section of rock, come up with a solution, and put it into practice very quickly." And so it is at Shelf Road. Labyrinthine cruxes, relentless angles beyond the vertical, and a seemingly endless resource of rock promise any type of climb imaginable. There is just one catch, however; most climbs hover in the stratosphere of difficulty. The potential for moderate climbing exists, but apparently no one is willing to develop it.

From the onset of development, climbers hungry for first ascents have sought out clean, difficult lines that even in the most developed areas have not been exhausted. Climbs that fire straight up bolted faces are viewed with intrigue rather than indignation. Shelf Road's limestone, when combined with an ethical bend toward sport climbing, breaks loose the shackles of blank rock and psychological limits of possibility. Time and again, ridiculously blank stretches of limestone give way to beautiful climbs. Routes such as *The Sabbatical* and *Skinwalker* on University Wall and The Mural on Mural Wall are examples of routes honored as "impossible lines" by myopic Shelf Road regulars. Shelf Road is not, to coin a phrase, "just another pretty face." While some faces, especially the jet black ones, are quite aesthetic, in general, Shelf Road limestone possesses little of the grandeur of the oceans of pocketed rock found in France.

But another axiom warns, "Don't judge a book by its cover". Even the climbs on Sand Gulch walls, formations apparently built by anti-climbing terrorists, can be incredible. Visitors are well advised to sample the many flavors of Shelf Road climbing. Climb in all the legal access areas to realize why many climbers recognize Shelf Road as one of the best sport climbing crags in the country.

While the methods of route development at Shelf Road still raise an occasional eyebrow, their value is now indisputable. The meticulously crafted climbs follow aesthetic lines that don't push out other possibilities; the clips are from sensible holds; and the lowering anchors are good. All this ensures that a high quality experience is enjoyed by all. In many ways, with the advent of climbing competitions and the "climbing out" of traditional crags, our future unfolds on steep sheets of well-bolted rock. As the local definition of difficulty stretches towards higher levels, it is possible that climbers who would never think of coming to an area top-heavy with difficult and extreme climbs may indeed experience an internal leap of faith to redefine their own personal limits.

DIRECTIONS

From U.S. Highway 50 in Canon City, locate Fields Avenue. (When coming into Canon City from the east, the first or second traffic light —Dozier and Raynolds, respectively—will get you to Fields Avenue. When coming in from the west, go through most of the town until you reach the traffic light at Raynolds.) Refer to the Canon City map to find your way out of town heading north on Fields Avenue. This road (Fremont County Road 9) travels about 12 miles to the climbing area and at that point becomes Shelf Road.

The designated start of Shelf Road is also the location of two entrances onto BLM land from which most climbing access begins. At the 9.5 mile mark of Fremont County Road 9, signs designate pullouts (gates or cattle guards) on the left

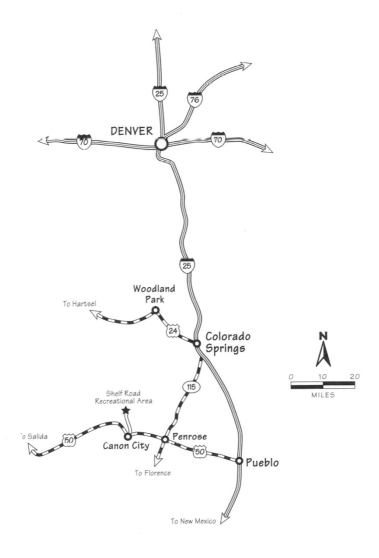

(west). The first pullout is Sand Gulch (including access to The Gallery) and the second is The Bank (including access to The Dark Side, and Dead Colt). Continue another 2 miles on Fremont County Road 9 (Shelf Road), to locate the trailhead for The Gymnasium (mile marker 12.25). The trail leaves the road on the left (west) and heads up the hillside. Note that this section of Shelf Road is closed to parking and continues to be so for another 2 miles (mile marker 14).

From the Sand Gulch gate, continue west 0.25 mile to the Sand Gulch Campground. From here, trails lead west to Sand Gulch (10 minutes), and south to The Gallery (20 minutes). The Bank road is followed 1.5 miles to The Bank Campground. Park here to approach trails in the eastern end of The Bank (10 minutes) and The Dark Side (15 minutes). The road forks just beyond the Day-Park area. The right fork leads directly into The Bank and can be driven another mile to access climbs at its western end. Note that this section of the road is closed to parking. The left fork (4WD recommended), is followed for another mile to Dead Colt. Take the road (south) into the canyon and park near (but not in) the stream bed.

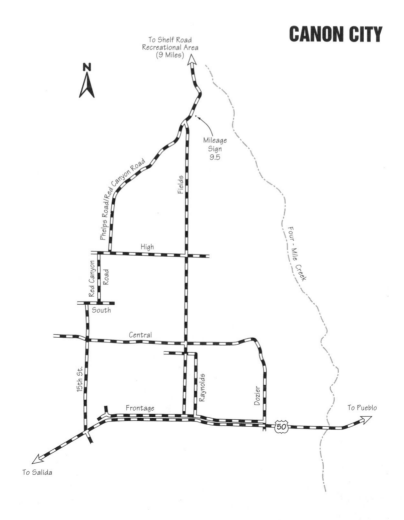

CANON CITY

INTRODUCTION

Shelf Road is a rock climbing area located in the foothills of south-central Colorado. A complex network of limestone canyons occupies pinon-juniper woodland along the historic Canon City-Cripple Creek stagecoach road known as Shelf Road. This limestone, combined with an ideal climate and a liberal bolting ethic, provides for an extensive collection of short, bolted, face climbs (i.e. sport climbs).

The continuing dissemination of free climbing has led to the development of many sport climbing areas in this country, yet none so refined as Shelf Road. The short cliffs of limestone provide a perfect medium for thin, technical face climbs. Close examination of the vertical and consistently featured rock reveals micro-edges, nubbins, and solution pockets ideal for difficult free climbing. The unrestrained yet thoughtful use of expansion bolts opens these imposing cliffs to the climber exclusively interested in the physical challenge provided through sport climbing. The variety and concentration of Shelf Road sport routes is unsurpassed. A dry and mild climate, reknowned in this part of Colorado, provides for year-round climbing opportunities, adding to the attraction of the Shelf Road area.

ARRANGEMENT OF THIS BOOK

The climbs covered in this book are separated into nine distinct areas, described geographically from the south to the north: The Gallery, Sand Gulch The Bank and The Vault are canyons, which are described in a clockwise (left to right) direction. Dead Colt, The Dark Side (north facing), Cactus Cliff, Spiney Ridge (south facing), and The Gymnasium (east facing) are single-aspect walls. When looking at any of the cliffs, descriptions travel from left to right.

Each area has a short, written introduction, followed by an overview map (or maps) showing campgrounds, parking areas, trails, main features and the locations of climbs. Black and white photos help to give a broader overview of the main walls of each area, while hand drawn topos give large scale overviews as well as the specific details. Be sure to remember that Shelf Road is a developing climbing area and there may very well be new climbs in between the routes you are looking for.

HISTORY

Considering that Shelf Road has seen the growth of several hundred routes in its relative short existence, its history is rich indeed. Throughout time, and up until the 1980s, the Shelf Road limestone was viewed as short, rotten, and not worth the time spent developing rock climbing routes. Prior to 1985, climbing activity was isolated and sporadic. It was in 1985 that a second wave of primarily "traditional" activity occurred, and paradoxically, this initiated a third wave of "European" development which has dominated the area ever since.

During the early 1980s, Harvey T. Carter visited the limestone crags at the north end of the current climbing areas. This area is known as The North End and contains a huge concentration of high quality jet, black limestone; unfortunately, it is on private property and is not open to rock climbing today. Carter established routes as well as spreading word of the limestone to other climbers who also visited The North End, such as Art and Earl Wiggins, Tom Eisenman, and Tom Austin. These climbers established several mixed free and aid routes in the traditional fashion, around 1983 and 1984. Later, in 1985, also at The North End, the first bolt route at Shelf Road was established. In traditional style, Charlie Fowler, Maureen Gallagher, Peter Gallagher, and Harvey Miller established *Limestone Cowboy*, placing three bolts and two pitons, via the lead, hanging on hooks to drill.

"Disgruntled Trads" at Shelf Road.

The beginning of large-scale route development began in January 1986, when climbers began establishing routes on what is now known as Cactus Cliff. Lying on the Shelf Road proper, Cactus Cliff is north from The Dark Side and is distinctly visible from The Bank campground/parking area. Cactus Cliff is open to rock climbing now. It was the starting point for the huge surge in route development at Shelf Road. Calling the area "Helena Canyon," Steve Cheney established many crack climbs with various partners, including Don Doucette, Kevin Murray, and Bill Blair. Most of these routes were in the 5.8 to 5.10 range. Routes such as *Crynoid Corner*, and *The Killer Toupee* generally ascended crack-and-corner systems. Cheney described the area in this manner: "The climbing is on limestone, which looks like brown dirt, 90 feet high."

In addition, Cheney visited the area with other climbers, such as Ric and Tom Geiman, Mike Johnson, and Lou Kalina, and word of the area's potential began to spread. Interest in face routes began when Johnson spotted a line at Cactus Cliff which was toproped. He later returned with Dale Goddard and established (on rappel) *Glue Slippage*, the first of what would be hundreds of sport routes at Shelf Road. At this same time, Johnson and Goddard also explored The Dark Side and established the routes *Mannequin* and *Line of Strength*. As the spring of 1986 rolled around, both Goddard and Johnson left the area, while other locals headed to the mountain crags of the Pikes Peak region.

Activity resumed late next fall as cooler weather returned. Kalina began visiting the area again, as did other climbers like Harvey Miller, Ed Quesada and Bob Robertson. Several more routes were established—mostly crack climbs—but a few bolted climbs went in as well. By the time winter came, the huge surge in activity was about to begin. Darryl Roth had heard of the Shelf Road limestone from several of Kalina's friends, and decided to visit the area with Richard Aschert, Dave Dangle, and Bob D'Antonio. At first the rock appeared loose and unconsolidated, but upon closer inspection, the faces revealed themselves to be clean, steep, and made for climbing on. The rush began. During the last two weeks of 1986, these climbers began to establish line after line of classic, bolted face routes at Cactus Cliff. Other climbers to become active during these early stages include Mark Milligan and Will Gadd.

Though the method was not yet perfected, these climbers adopted a top-down approach for establishing routes. Possible lines were toproped to work out moves and to decide where to place the bolts. After a consensus was reached, bolts were placed on toprope and then the climb was redpointed. Routes established during this period include *The French Are Here*, *New Ethics*, and *Hot Beach*.

In addition to activities at Cactus Cliff, locals explored the area for other possibilities. At the beginning of 1987, Roth discovered The Bank and, together with Dangle and Aschert, found Sand Gulch, University Wall, and finally The Gallery. The first routes established in The Bank included *Unusual Weather*, *Back to the Future*, *Taping Tendons* and *Living In America*.

Unfortunately, as rock climbing activity increased at Cactus Cliff, the land owner became concerned over the issue of liability and effectively stopped climbers from using his property. Roth researched the situation with the (Bureau of Land Management) BLM to establish public property boundaries, in order to determine how much rock was possible for exploration. All rock located north of The Bank was thought to be on private property, and rock climbing activity became limited to the new areas recently discovered south of Cactus Cliff.

With activity focused on public lands, it continued at an industrious level. When Aschert became the first climber in the area to purchase a battery operated, hammer-rotary drill, in April 1987, several routes were being established in a single day. In honor of the new technology, Aschert established *Welcome to the Machine*. During this time, most routes being established were in the shady areas of The Bank and University Wall. For the sport climber, this transitional period from hand-drilling to the use of the

Private lands at Shelf Road are closed to rockclimbing. This situation has improved dramatically in 1999.

BLM signs with Shelf Road information.

Bosch strengthened Shelf Road's appeal. Two-bolt lowering stations slowly became common, as did a liberal approach to placing bolts (by first ascent parties). There is a subtle but distinct difference in character between the "pre" and "post" Bosch-day rock climbs.

The cooler weather in the fall of 1987 brought the focus of rock climbing activity to the left side of Sand Gulch. Routes established here include *The Apple Bites Back*, *Metropolis*, and *Little Mecca*. By the end of spring 1988, multiple routes existed on both sides of the canyon. As the warmer temperatures of summer 1988 began, activity spread to other areas, including The Dark Side and also a new canyon to the south of Sand Gulch called The Gallery. In The Gallery, Roth and Aschert established the first of what was to eventually be six routes on Mural Wall. Roth also completed his first 5.13 route, *Chomping At the Bit*, on the shady side of The Gallery.

Other activists began to visit Shelf Road regularly, including Mark Van Horn, Glenn Schuler, Byron Dacus, Charles Walters, Brian Mullin, Paul Piana, Dan Michael, and Bobbi Bensman. At this time, perhaps as many as a half-dozen climbers equipped with power drills were visiting Shelf Road frequently. Previously established routes also felt the influx of so many activists. More lowering stations appeared and bolts began to eliminate the need to carry "clean" gear.

During the spring of 1988, Roth and Van Horn initiated exploration of The Gymnasium, located in Helena Canyon and overlooking Shelf Road. The first routes established here include *VHS or BETA* and *I Never Met A Carbo I Didn't Like*. Property boundaries at this time were not particularly well defined and it appeared that this huge, east-facing crag was open to rock climbing. Colin Lantz was quick to establish *The Example*, one of Shelf Road's most impressive lines. However, as activity at this area heightened, pressure from a local land owner increased to close the cliff. At one point, climbers were dispersed by a Fremont County Sheriffs Department official. Also making the access situation more problematic was the county-instituted parking closure of the rugged four-mile section of road through the canyon. In effect, these events halted any rock climbing activity at that time.

By the end of the 1980s the large majority of Shelf Road's limestone had been explored. Route development by this time had moderated, as the potential was becoming limited. However, increasingly large numbers of climbers were beginning to make use of Shelf Road's generous selection of new, bolted face climbs. Other activists who had visited the area included Dan Durland, Paul Lanz, Kerry Gunter, Kevin McLaughlin, Bill Schmausser, Kevin Gonzales, Eric Harp, Eric Johnson, Jon Lawyer, Larry Harris, Curt Fry, and Gary Bratten. Many original routes experienced acts of retro-bolting to bring them up to current "sport climbing" standards.

The first guidebook to Shelf Road became available in late 1990. Ensuring an out-of-date volume before availability, new route activity surged. In The Gallery, Kurt Smith established several routes before becoming active at Rifle in western Colorado. Also in The Gallery, *Period Piece* was established by Julie Fredlund and Charles Tabor. This is an excellent moderate route on the Menses Prow. Other climbers involved in new route development at this time included Mike Pont, Carrie Robertson, John Herzog, Kemper Knight, and Erick Christianson.

As Shelf Road was becoming such a popular rock climbing area, the need to mitigate human impact was met by the Colorado Springs-based American Mountain Foundation (AMF). Joining together in a partnership with the Canon City BLM Office, the AMF organized meetings and surveys to establish rock climbers' goals for the area. The AMF also conducted trail inventories for future trail development. Formal trail work utilizing volunteer support began by 1992 and has continued regularly until the present time. Also resulting from this partnership has been the addition of two well-planned primitive campgrounds in 1996. The success of this BLM/AMF partnership is testimony to what can be accomplished when channels of communication are opened to all concerned groups and initiative is taken to *direct* the future of a recreational area. In recognition of the AMF's outstanding efforts, they received the Department of the Interior's "Take Pride In America" award. In 1998 the AMF changed its name to the Rocky Mountain Field Institute, but fortunately will continue to be instrumental in the ongoing maintenance of the area.

With limestone resources becoming exhausted, local climbers once again looked to The Gymnasium and elsewhere for potential new routes. As a result of increased use beginning again around 1995, the local land owner requested official land surveys be done to create definitive property lines. The completed survey revealed that The Gymnasium's entire left side (south of *The Example*) was private property not open to rock climbing. The right side of this cliff is BLM property, extending north for about 1 mile from the trailhead, and open to public use. Approximately half of Shelf Road's limestone is open to rock climbing. As more rock becomes available to the public, this already highly developed area will become increasingly important as a recreational rock climbing area.

In recent years, new route activity has slowed; however, new lines are nevertheless being opened. Sand Gulch and The Gallery have had the largest number of routes developed, while The Dark Side and The Bank have seen additions as well. Most newer routes appear on the shorter-but-more-difficult—or longer and moderate—faces and cracks that were overlooked in the past years. Developers of the latest routes at Shelf Road include Ed Schmitt, Rick Thompson, Jeff Bates, Mike Sheldon, Azenda Cater, and Pat Thompson

Throughout the 1990s, rock climbing activity has continued at each of the individual areas with some degree of frequency, though most classic lines seem to have already been established. As stated above, the limited future of route development will take place on the longer, moderate faces and cracks, and the short—though aesthetic—bulges and faces that exist.

With the amount of unclimbed rock diminishing, the importance of developing quality routes becomes foremost. Regardless of how Shelf Road develops in the future, its past has without question brought rock climbers one of the finest crags in the country.

ABOUT THE ROCKY MOUNTAIN FIELD INSTITUTE

Rocky Mountain Field Institute

The Rocky Mountain Field Institute (formerly the American Mountain Foundation) is a non-profit organization based in Colorado Springs, CO. The organization is dedicated to the preservation and restoration of mountains, wildlands, and other key natural areas. RMFI completes projects that focus on mitigating human disturbances and preserving and restoring the natural partnership with city, state, and federal land management agencies. RMFI projects are completed through one or more of the following programs: field research, secondary and under-graduate field study courses, academic internships, volunteer service programs, and special contract work. The Rocky Mountain Field Institute has developed a number of highly successful projects, including: the Colorado Fourteeners Initiative, the Eldorado Canyon Trails Project, the Shelf Road Recreation Area Project, and the Indian Creek Canyon Preservation Project. RMFI is supported by charitable organizations, businesses, and individuals. To find out more about the organization, contact the Rocky Mountain Field Institute (see Appendix).

ACCESS/RESTRICTIONS

All of the recreational areas covered in this book are managed by the Bureau of Land Management (BLM). Many rules and regulations are in place at The Shelf Road Recreation Area. Persons interested in all of these regulations may obtain further information by contacting the BLM office in Canon City (see Appendix).

In order for rock climbers to maintain a positive relationship with the BLM, it is important to familiarize yourself with the regulations in effect. Key regulations for rock climbers include: using *established* climbing areas, campgrounds, parking areas, roads, and trails. Keep gates closed or open (as you find them) after passing through them. Further more, bring your own water and pack out everything you pack in. Our activities at Shelf Road are closely observed by the BLM as well as the local community, and it is therefore important for rock climbers to conduct themselves in a responsible manner to ensure continued access.

CAMPING

Camping in the area is permitted with a $4.00/night fee ($8.00/night for group sites) and there are limited services. BLM regulations are in effect and are posted at both Sand Gulch and The Bank Campground registers, or the BLM office in Canon City. Remember, there is no water, and—as always—"if you pack it in, pack it out." Both areas get early morning sun; however, the Sand Gulch area seems to be better sheltered from the wind. If you have fires, use wood sparingly (bring your own) and use existing fire rings. Never leave fires unattended.

AMENITIES

All modern amenities, including water, food, gasoline, restaurants, liquor, lodging, etc., are found in Canon City. Gambling is possible in Cripple Creek.

Rock climbing equipment is available in Colorado Springs at The Mountain Chalet (see Appendix). Indoor climbing and rock climbing guide services are also available in Colorado Springs at The Sport Climbing Center (see Appendix).

LOCAL HAZARDS

Several hazards, natural and unnatural, exist at Shelf Road.

Dangerous Critters: Though not common, rattlesnakes can be found in the area, as can scorpions. The tall and spiny cholla cactus is wisely avoided, as is the poison ivy occasionally encountered. Staying on trails can help minimize the likelihood of an ugly situation.

Flooding—Climb to Safety: The dry creek beds at the bottoms of the canyons can experience periods of flash flooding during rainstorms. Camping or parking in the creek beds is not advised.

Dangerous Locals: The climber should also be aware that the area is popular with hunters. Turkey and deer seasons (April and October, respectively), bring the majority of activity. Other hunting seasons exist as well. Check with the BLM for further information. During these times, bright-colored clothing is an intelligent choice.

ETHICS/SAFETY

Though sport climbing is viewed by some to be a black hole of ethics, some rules have become recognized. Route development is done with the utmost concern for those who will follow *after* you. The goal when establishing a new route is to place bolts in such a manner that the leader of the route only concerns herself/himself with the actual climbing. Objective danger is out, subjective difficulty is in. Routes are done almost exclusively using a "top-down" method. Some climbs have been done on the lead, but remember it is your responsibility to create a route that can be enjoyed by all. As long as the final result is a good route, bolt as you see fit. All hardware used should be commercially available bolts, hangers, and chains. The intermittent use of clean gear (stoppers, hexes, Friends, etc.) is generally not advised. Due to the extreme case-hardening of the limestone, seemingly bombproof protection is likely to fail. The use of clean gear also tends to give the first ascent party an unfair advantage. (Climbs utilizing clean gear tend to be retro-bolted in order to make them "clip and go" anyway.)

Finally, a lowering station at the end of a route has become standard procedure, rather than taking climbs over the top of the cliff. Two-and three-point, all-metal anchors are fundamentally the best choice. Retro-bolting in the interest of the free climbing community is generally accepted. Be as clean as possible and be sure you have a consensus behind you when you feel a change is necessary.

Virtually all routes at Shelf Road are set up to be a climbed and descended using a single 165-foot rope. There are exceptions, however, so know your descent plan before starting up any route.

Mark Van Horn on Thirteen Engines.

Other obvious ethics should also be observed. Don't trash out the area and pick up after those who have been more careless. Use trails and respect the fragile environment in which you climb. Deposit human waste more than a foot or two away from the cliffs and trails, and try using a stick to wipe! And most importantly, remember that our greatest moments of satisfaction in climbing occur when we are being honest with ourselves. Climb, respect, and enjoy.

BOULDERING

Bouldering is possible at Shelf Road, though not concentrated. While each area may have a few boulders, The Gallery tends to have the largest number. Traverses across some of the major walls in the canyons also provide bouldering opportunities. A small but good selection of Dakota Sandstone boulders can be found at about the 2.5 mile marker on Fremont County Road 9 (Garden Park) as you travel towards the climbing areas. As a landmark, a large pipeline runs through the area. Some devoted bouldering enthusiasts have explored the area, yet it usually appears that at Shelf Road, if there is time for bouldering, then there is time for climbing.

RATINGS

When I first began working on the guidebook to Shelf Road my intention was to make a statement about the "sport" nature of route development here. In order to set the area apart from other U.S. crags, I thought the exclusive use of the French grading system would make this statement. However, to avoid some degree of confusion, both U.S. and French grades appear with each climb, as well as a conversion chart to clarify the relationship between the two systems. The French system is less specific in its particular grades, and works better for most routes in this type of area, due to the wide variety of variables involved (i.e. experience, height, body size, sequence, chalk on holds etc.)

In terms of route seriousness, Shelf Road is ideally protected. Routes have been established with the goal of placing bolts in such a manner that the leader is never aware of protection (i.e. leaving her/him to contemplate the actual moves of the route). On routes where this goal has not been achieved, an "s" (serious) or "vs" (very serious)

U.S. – FRENCH CONVERSION CHART

U.S.	French	U.S.	French
.6+	4	.12a	7a
.7	4	.12a/b	7a+
.7+	4	.12b	7b
.8	5	.12b/c	7b
.8+	5	.12c	7b+
.9	5	.12c/d	7c
.9+	5+	.12d	7c
.10a	5+	.12d/.13a	7c
.10a/b	6a	.13a	7c+
.10b	6a	.13a/b	8a
.10b/c	6a	.13b	8a
.10c	6a+	.13b/c	8a
.10c/d	6b	.13c	8a+
.10d	6b	.13c/d	8b
.10d / 11a	6b	.13d	8b
.11a	6b	.13d/.14a	8b
.11a/b	6b+	.14a	8b+
.11b	6c	.14a/b	8c
.11b/c	6c	.14b	8c
.11c	6c	.14b/c	8c
.11c/d	6c+	.14c	8c+
.11d	7a	.14c/d	9a
.11d/.12a	7a	.14d	9a

suffix has been placed next to the grade. The leaders of "s" suffix routes should be more comfortable at the specific grades they are attempting. Falls on routes with the "s" suffix will generally not be dangerous, but may be longer than on routes without. For routes with serious consequences in the event of a fall, a "vs" suffix follows the grade. The "s" or "vs" suffix also indicates the possibility of unsound rock on that particular route. Usually a visual inspection will confirm whether or not this is the case. Absence of these suffixes *probably* indicates a safe route. However, once you are on the rock, your own judgement is the key to safety; you are on your own.

To benefit those with a limited amount of time in the area, a three star quality system is utilized. Zero stars indicates a poor or lesser quality route, while three stars indicates a high quality route. Because these are the most subjective of the ratings, many climbers will find routes with no stars to be their personal favorites, while others will find three star routes quite awful. The star ratings are simply the author's opinion of a route's quality; use them as you may.

Some climbs have been established as topropes and are indicated as such by "tr only" after the grades. Due to technical difficulties, such as loose rock or dangerous fall potential, some routes have not been equipped with bolts; however, toprope anchors exist, allowing these routes to be enjoyed with a greater margin of safety.

Remember that the ratings on some climbs at Shelf Road are relatively new and have not yet solidified. Use them as an approximation of the difficulties just make sure you can see the holds on the route you would like to attempt.

MAP LEGEND

Interstate		Cabins/Buildings/	
US Highway		Topography	
State or Other Principal Road		Gate	
Interstate Highway		Mine Site	
Paved Road		Railroad	
Gravel Road		County Line Boundary	
Unimproved Road		Continental Divide	
Trailhead		Fence Line	
Main Trail(s) /Route(s)		Powerline	
Bushwhack		Snowfield	
Parking Area		Glacier	
River/Creek/Waterfall		Map Orientation	
County Road	CR	N	
Forest Road	FR		
Forest Trail	FT		
Four Wheel Drive	4WD		
Two Wheel Drive	2WD	Scale	0 0.5 1
Campground			Miles

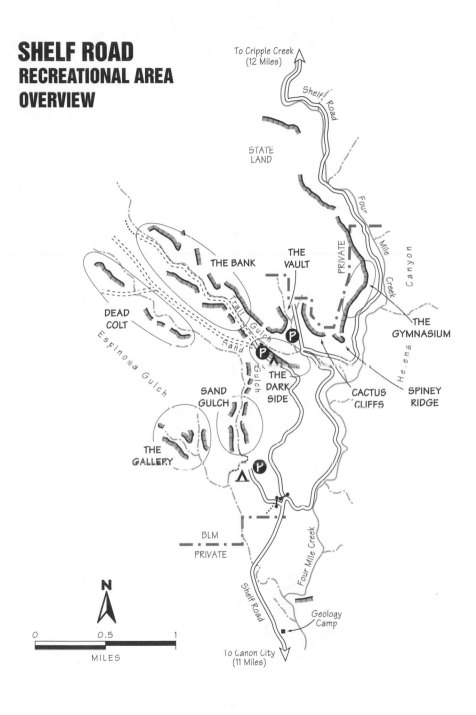

SHELF ROAD
RECREATIONAL AREA
OVERVIEW

To Cripple Creek
(12 Miles)

Shelf Road

STATE
LAND

Four Mile Creek

Canyon

PRIVATE

THE BANK

THE VAULT

THE
GYMNASIUM

DEAD
COLT

Trail Gulch

Sand Gulch

Espinosa Gulch

He-ena Creek

SAND
GULCH

THE
DARK
SIDE

CACTUS
CLIFFS

SPINEY
RIDGE

THE
GALLERY

BLM
PRIVATE

Four Mile Creek

Shelf Road

Geology
Camp

To Canon City
(11 Miles)

N

0   0.5   1

MILES

THE GALLERY AND SAND GULCH OVERVIEW

THE GALLERY

SAND GULCH

Far Side

Menses Prow

Mural Wall

Contest Wall

Freeform Wall

County 9

Sand Gulch
BLM Campground

P

Shelf Road Limestone provides interesting features and spectacular positions. Climber: Dave Dangle

TOPO LEGEND

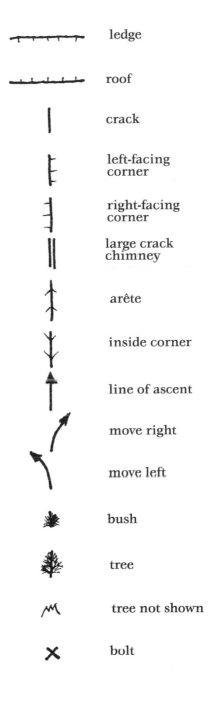

ledge

roof

crack

left-facing corner

right-facing corner

large crack chimney

arête

inside corner

line of ascent

move right

move left

bush

tree

tree not shown

bolt

THE GALLERY (BLM)

The Gallery is a canyon that branches in the middle and forms climbs on both sides as well as on a central buttress. The left (south) side features The Farside and The Pitts; these areas contain a number of climbs on high quality black rock. The central buttress is Menses Prow, named after the prominent red wall visible from the canyon's entrance. Menses Prow offers a large variety of rock types, from the sandstone-like rock on the front (east) side, to the hard, pocketed rock on either the north or south sides. On the right (north) side of the canyon lies the incredible Mural Wall, with its perfect, white, polished limestone. Other climbs on darker rock exist to the left of Mural Wall as well. The scenery and variety of The Gallery add to the charm of this extensive area.

GALLERY-SAND GULCH
OVERVIEW

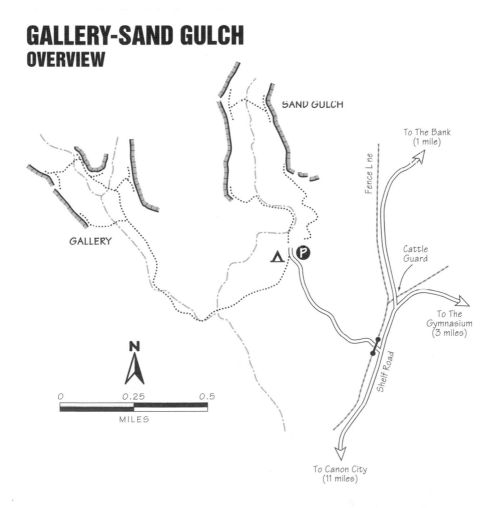

To reach The Gallery, locate a sign and trailhead between Sites 9 and 10 in the Sand Gulch Campground. Follow this trail to the next canyon south of Sand Gulch; this is The Gallery.

For climbs on the left (south) side of the canyon, (Far Side and Pitts) continue on the main trail near the creek bed until it breaks left and uphill. This is the Far Side trail, and it is marked with a sign. For climbs on the right side of the canyon (Mural Wall) as well as the central buttress (Menses Prow), take the Mural Wall trail, which is also marked by a sign and branches off to the right. This trail eventually splits, with the right branch leading to Mural Wall and the left branch leading to Menses Prow.

A hike up the creek bed also serves as access to The Gallery (passing through The Impact Zone) but does contain some poison ivy. Approach time: 20-30 minutes.

GALLERY

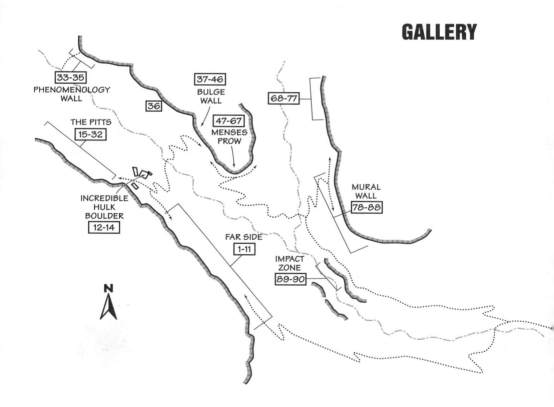

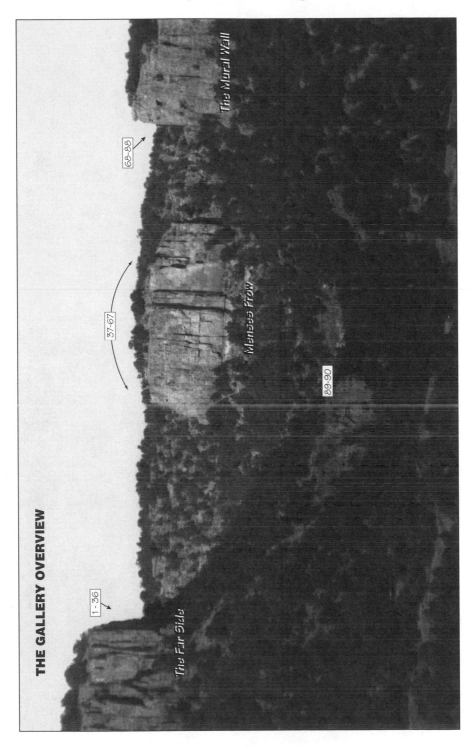

THE GALLERY OVERVIEW

1 - 36

37-67

68-88

89-90

The Far Side

Menses Prow

The Mural Wall

THE FAR SIDE

1   *Lizard With A View 5.11c/d (6c+)* ★★
2   *Big Lizard In My Backyard 5.11b/c (6c)* ★
4   *Black Is Beautiful 5.12d (7c)* ★★
6   *Unknown 5.11c (6c)* ★

THE FAR SIDE

1   *Lizard With A View 5.11c/d (6c+)* ★★
4   *Black Is Beautiful 5.12d (7c)* ★★

TRAIL

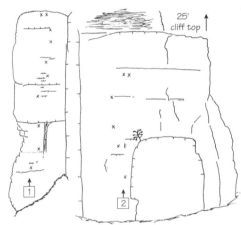

THE GALLERY
Southwest side

THE FAR SIDE

1 **Lizard With A View**
5.11c/d (6c+) ★★
Sustained, good rock.

2 **Big Lizard In My
Backyard** 5.11b/c (6c) ★

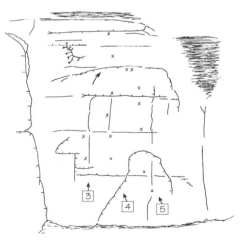

3 **Iguana Breath** 5.11a/b (6b+) ★

4 **Black Is Beautiful** 5.12d (7c) ★★
Thin, reaches.

5 **Thick As Thieves** 5.12a (7a) ★★
Hard start, good rock.

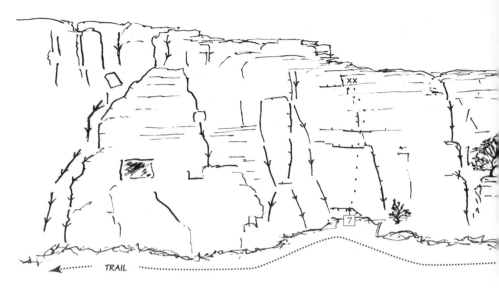

TRAIL

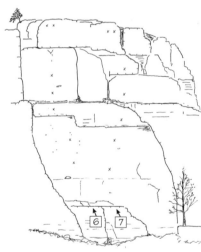

6   Unknown 5.11c (6c) ★

7   Lord Of The Warlocks 5.11c (6c)

8   Exorcist 5.11c (6c) ★

9   Satan's Revenge 5.11a (6b)

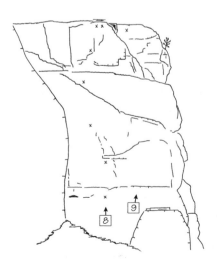

THE FAR SIDE

7 *Lord Of The Warlocks 5.11c (6c)*
8 *Exorcist 5.11c (6c)* ★
10 *Not A Girly Kinda Guy 5.11b (6c)*
11 *Sympathy For The Devil 5.11a (6b)*

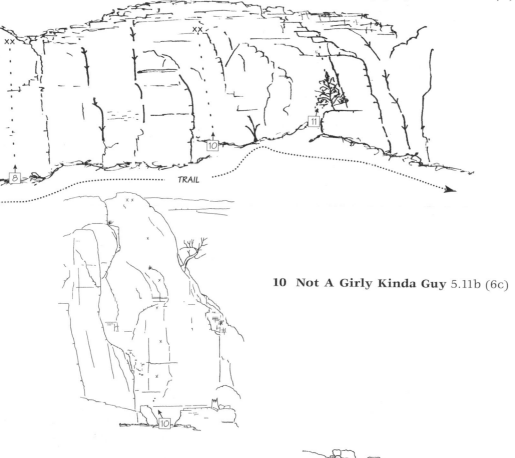

TRAIL

10 Not A Girly Kinda Guy 5.11b (6c)

11 Sympathy For The Devil 5.11a (6b)

INCREDIBLE HULK
BOULDER

12 Somatophrique Physique 5.12b (7b) ★
Power moves, reaches.

13 Super Phrique 5.13a (7c+) ★
Thin, power moves.

14 The Mutant 5.11d (7a) ★
Power moves.

Mark Van Horn on Somatophrique Physique 5.12b (7b)

THE PITTS

15 *Well Hung 5.11d (7a)* ★★
18 *Abracadabra 5.9 (5)* ★★
23 *Come And Get It 5.12d/5.13a (7c)* ★
26 *Just Out Shootin' Blanks 5.11b (6c)* ★★

THE DUNGEON

26 *The Dungeon Crack 5.11b (6c)* ★
29 *Remoat Control 5.11c (6c)* ★

THE PITTS

15 *Well Hung 5.11d (7a)* ★★
17 *Flight Of The Monarch 5.11b (6c)* ★
18 *Abracadabra 5.9 (5)* ★★
21 *Chomping At The Bit 5.13b (8a)* ★★★
26 *Just Out Shootin' Blanks 5.11b (6c)* ★★

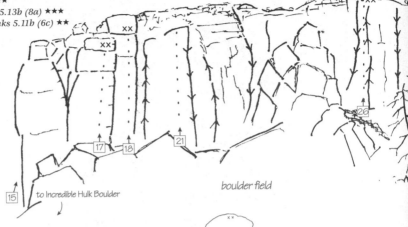

to Incredible Hulk Boulder

boulder field

THE PITTS

15 **Well Hung** 5.11d (7a) ★★
   Strenuous.

16 **Unknown** 5.11d (7a)
   Squeezed.

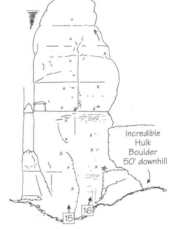

Incredible
Hulk
Boulder
50' downhill

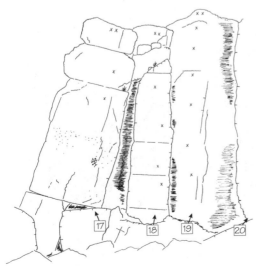

17 **Flight Of The Monarch**
   5.11b (6c) ★
   Good rock.

18 **Abracadabra** 5.9 (5) ★★
   Good rock.

19 **In The Reign Of The Butterfly Pump** ★ 5.11a/b (6b+)

THE DUNGEON

28 *The Dungeon Crack 5.11b (6c)* ★
29 *Remoat Control 5.11c (6c)* ★
32 *Dragon Fire 5.10b (6a)*

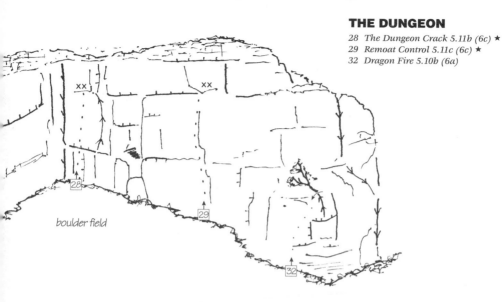

boulder field

20 Elvis Is Everywhere 5.10b (6a)

21 Chomping At The Bit 5.13b (8a) ★★★
Technical, deceptive.

22 I Can Smell Your Thoughts 5.11c (6c) ★
Strenuous, sharp.

23 Come And Get It 5.12d/5.13a (7c) ★
Very thin

24 Elusive Minos 5.11d (7a)
Sustained, sharp.

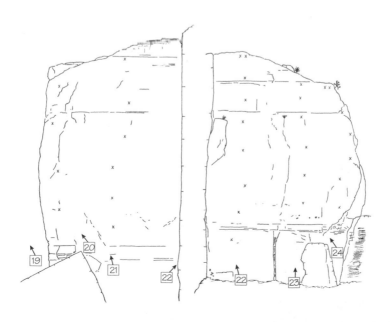

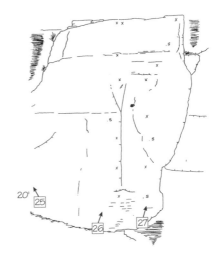

25 Third Generation 5.10a (5+)
Three bolts. Short black bulge.

26 Just Out Shootin' Blanks 5.11b
(6c) ★★
Good rock, devious.

27 The Spider 5.12a s (7a) ★

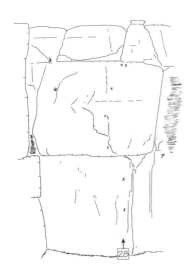

THE DUNGEON

28 The Dungeon Crack 5.11b (6c) ★
Crack to thin face.

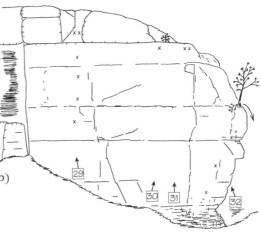

29 Remoat Control 5.11c (6c) ★
Thin, continuous.

30 Clear The Decks 5.12d (7c)
TR only.

31 The Chopping Block 5.10d (6b)
TR only.

32 Dragon Fire 5.10b (6a)
Short, reaches.

THE GALLERY
Central Buttress

PHENOMENOLOGY WALL

33 Armies Of Metaphors 5.11c (6c) ★
Thin, devious.

34 Abscessed Words To Climb 5.11a
(6b) ★★
Good rock, pockets.

35 Metaphysical Fictions 5.11b (6c) ★

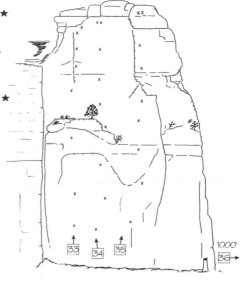

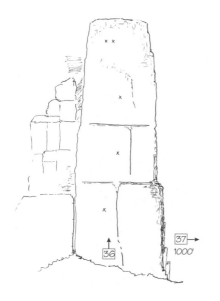

36 Unknown 5.10d (6b)

BULGE WALL

37 *Turbo Charged, Inter-Cooled, Meat Machine 5.10c/d (6b)* ★★
41 *Thirteen Engines 5.11d (7a)* ★★
46 *Dumb Waiter 5.9+ (5+)* ★
48 *Slender Fungus 5.10d (6b)* ★

CALIFORNIA ETHICS PINNACLE

53 *Nouveau Tradition 5.7 (4)*

BULGE WALL

37 *Turbo Charged, Inter-Cooled, Meat Machine 5.10c/d (6b)* ★★
40 *My What A Big Bulge 5.11d (7a)* ★★
43 *Lick My Love Pump 5.10b/c (6a)* ★
46 *Dumb Waiter 5.9+ (5+)* ★

48 *Slender Fungus 5.10d (6b)* ★

CALIFORNIA ETHICS PINNACLE

53 *Nouveau Tradition 5.7 (4)*

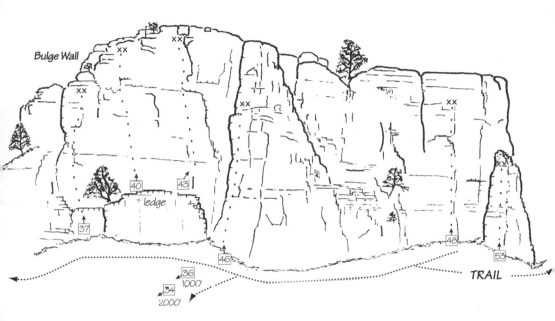

BULGE WALL

37 Turbo Charged, Inter-Cooled, Meat Machine 5.10c/d (6b) ★★
Strenuous, reaches.

38 Pig Dictionary 5.12a/b (7a+) ★★
Good rock, very thin.

39 Stratabulge 5.12b (7b) ★★
Good rock, thin, reaches.

40 My What A Big Bulge 5.11d (7a) ★★
Thin, sharp.

41 Thirteen Engines 5.11d (7a) ★★
Strenuous.

42 Liquid Affair 5.11b (6c) ★
Thin, brief crux.

43 Lick My Love Pump 5.10b/c (6a) ★

44 Jumbo Pumping Love 5.10d (6b) ★

BULGE WALL

37   *Turbo Charged, Inter-Cooled, Meat*
         Machine 5.10c/d (6b) ★★
38   *Pig Dictionary 5.12a/b (7a+)* ★★
39   *Stratabulge 5.12b (7b)* ★★
40   *My What A Big Bulge 5.11d (7a)* ★★
41   *Thirteen Engines 5.11d (7a)* ★★
42   *Liquid Affair 5.11b (6c)* ★
43   *Lick My Love Pump 5.10b/c (6a)* ★
44   *Jumbo Pumping Love 5.10d (6b)* ★
45   *The B.O.S.S. Method 5.8 (5)*

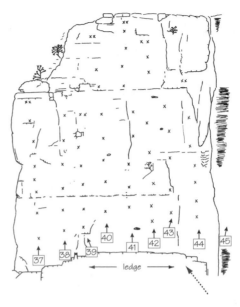

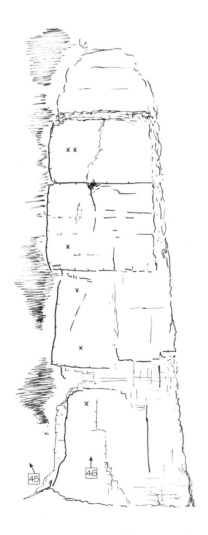

45   The B.O.S.S. Method 5.8 (5)

46   Dumb Waiter 5.9+ (5+) ★

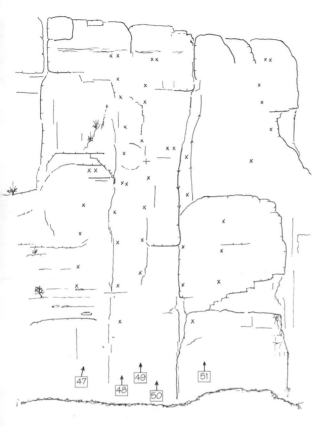

47 **Flashback To Acid Beach** 5.10c (6a+) ★

48 **Slender Fungus** 5.10d (6b) ★

49 **Graceland** 5.11c s (6c) ★

50 **Unknown** 5.10b/c (6a)
    Crack.

51 **Unknown** 5.11d (7a)

CALIFORNIA ETHICS PINNACLE

52 **True To Tradition** 5.7 (4)

53 **Nouveau Tradition** 5.7 (4)

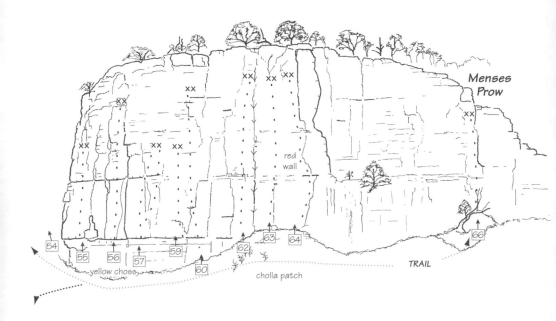

MENSES PROW

54 *Period Piece 5.8 (5)* ★★★
55 *Unknown 5.12a s (7a)* ★
56 *Unknown 5.11d (5) / 12a (7a)* ★★
57 *Unknown 5.11c (6c)* ★★
59 *Sundogs 5.12a/b (7a+)* ★★
60 *No Passion For Fashion 5.11b/c (6c)* ★★★
62 *Lunch At The Y 5.11b/c (6c)* ★★
63 *Menses 5.10d (6b)* ★★
64 *The Big Chill 5.10c (6a+)* ★
66 *Fever 5.11b (6c)* ★★

Mark Mitten on The Big Chill 5.10c (6a+) .

MENSES PROW

54 *Period Piece 5.8 (5)* ★ ★ ★
56 *Unknown 5.11d (5) / 12a (7a)* ★ ★
60 *No Passion For Fashion 5.11b / c (6c)* ★ ★ ★
62 *Lunch at the Y 5.10c (6a+)* ★
64 *The Big Chill 5.11b / c (6c)* ★ ★
65 *Swarm Rider 5.11b (6c)* ★ ★

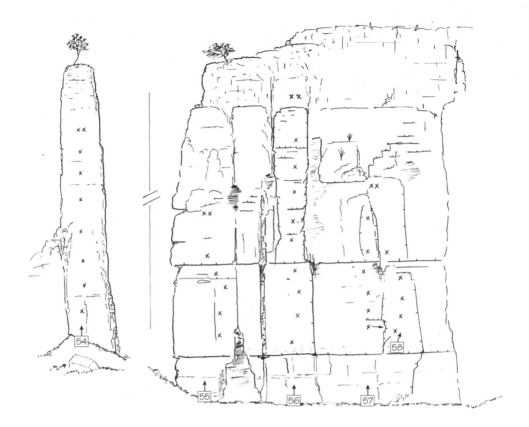

MENSES PROW

54 Period Piece 5.8 (5) ★★★
Good rock, sustained.

55 Unknown 5.12a s (7a) ★
Loose.

56 Unknown 5.11d/5.12a (7a) ★★
Squeezed, good position.

57 Unknown 5.11c (6c) ★★

58 Unknown 5.11d s (7a) ★

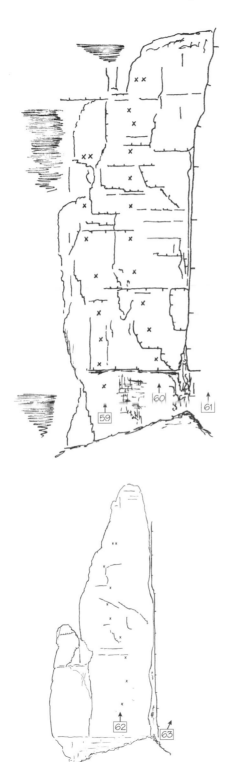

59 Sundogs 5.12a/b (7a+) ★★
Devious.

60 No Passion For Fashion 5.11b/c
(6c) ★★★
Strenuous.

61 This Nuts For You 5.10c vs (6a+)
Pro to 3". Thin crack system.

62 Lunch At The Y 5.11b/c (6c) ★★

63 Menses 5.10d (6b) ★★
Continuous, sloping.

64 The Big Chill 5.10c (6a+) ★

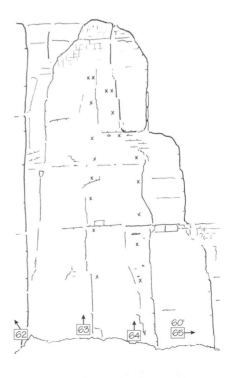

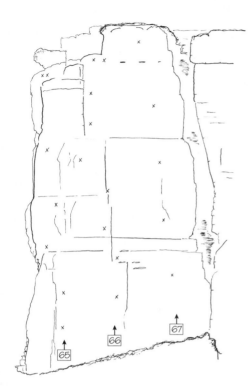

65 Storm Rider 5.11b (6c) ★★

66 Fever 5.11b (6c) ★★

67 Delirium 5.12a s (7a) ★

THE GALLERY
Northeast Side

68 Bullet This! 5.11b (6c)
Three bolts, short black bulge.

69 Living In A Vacuum 5.10c (6a+) ★
Continuous.

70 Call To Arms 5.11d/5.12a (7a) ★★
Roofs, good position.

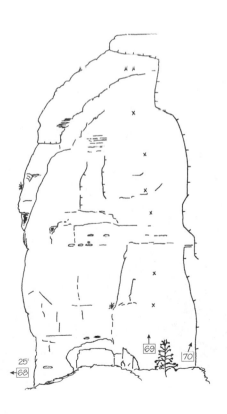
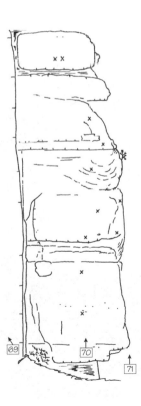

THE GALLERY - NORTHEAST SIDE

69 *Living In A Vacuum 5.10c (6a+)* ★
71 *Sea of Joy 5.11c (6c)* ★
74 *Wading Through A Ventilator 5.11b (6c)* ★★
78 *M & M 5.12a (7a)* ★★
80 *Mosaic 5.12b/c (7b)* ★★★
83 *Motif 5.12a (7a)* ★★
84 *Morrocan Roll 5.10b (6a)* ★
86 *The Bobbit Effect 5.9+ (5+)* ★

THE GALLERY - NORTHEAST SIDE

70 *Call To Arms 5.11d/5.12a (7a)* ★★
76 *Tuna!, Tuna!, Tuna! 5.11b/c (6c)* ★

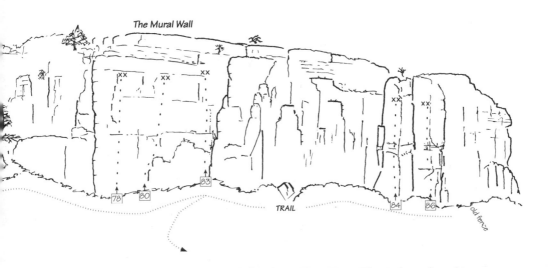

The Mural Wall

71 **Sea Of Joy** 5.11c (6c) ★

72 **Dolphin Dancing** 5.11c (6c) ★

73 **Have A Blast** 5.12a (7a) ★★
Sequential.

74 **Wading Through A
Ventilator** 5.11b (6c) ★★

75 **Happy Nightmare Baby** 5.10b
(6a) ★

76 **Tuna!, Tuna!, Tuna!** 5.11b/c
(6c) ★
Good rock, roofs.

77 **Soluble Fish** 5.11b/c (6c) ★
Good rock, roofs.

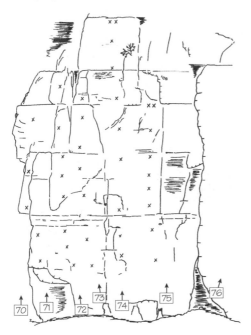

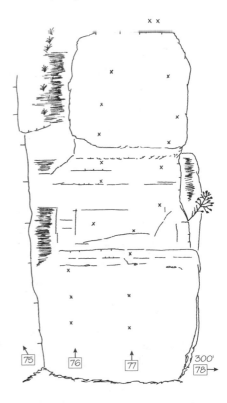

THE MURAL WALL

78 M & M 5.12a (7a) ★★
82 Monet 5.11d (7a) ★★
84 Morridean Roll 5.10b (6a) ★
83 John Cruiser Meloncrimp 5.10b (6a) ★★

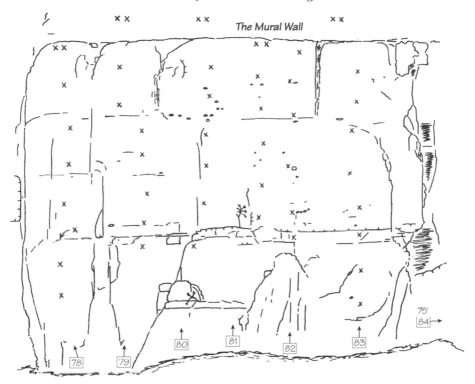

The Mural Wall

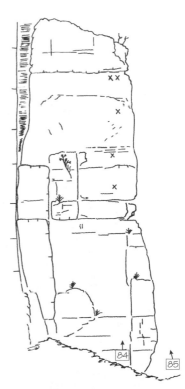

THE MURAL WALL

78 **M & M** 5.12a (7a) ★★
Thin.

79 **Montage** 5.12d (7c) ★★
Very thin.

80 **Mosaic** 5.12b/c (7b) ★★★
Great rock, very thin.

81 **The Mural** 5.12a/b (7a+) ★★★
Great rock, sustained, pockets.

82 **Monet** 5.11d (7a) ★★
Great rock, sequential, pockets.

83 **Motif** 5.12a (7a) ★★
Great rock, sequential, pockets.

84 **Morrocan Roll** 5.10b (6a) ★

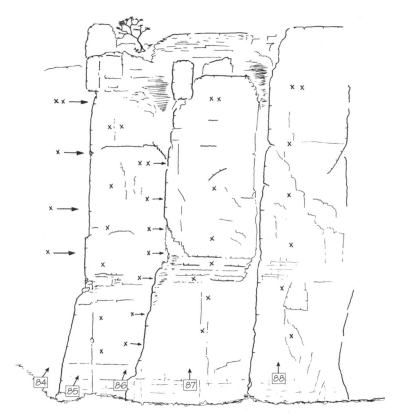

85 Mother Of Invention 5.10c (6a+/b) ★

86 The Bobbit Effect 5.9+ (5+) ★

87 Pi 5.12a (7a) ★★

88 John Cruiser Meloncrimp 5.10b (6a) ★★

THE IMPACT ZONE

89 Predator Party 5.12a (7a) ★
Rappel start.

90 Sudden Impact 5.11a (6b) ★
Rappel start.

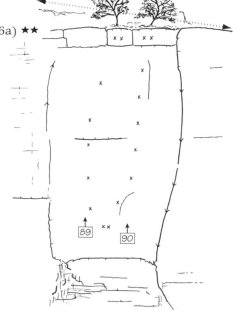

Mark Van Horn on Sudden Impact 5.11a (6b).

SAND GULCH (BLM)

Sand Gulch hosts a large selection of climbs and a wide variety of rock types. Some black rock is found; however, pocketed, sandstone-like rock is more abundant. With its easy access, Sand Gulch is very popular for climbing and camping.

From the Sand Gulch Campground you look directly north into the canyon. A sign designates the trailhead that leads into Sand Gulch. Follow the creek bed upstream until you get to two trailheads leading to either side of the canyon. Signs designate each of these trailheads. The Contest Wall trail is encountered first and is on the left. The Freeform Wall trail is 0.25 mile beyond on the right. The east side of Sand Gulch (Freeform Wall) may also be approached from a trailhead located in the group site of Sand Gulch Campground. Approach time: 10 to 20 minutes.

GALLERY-SAND GULCH
OVERVIEW

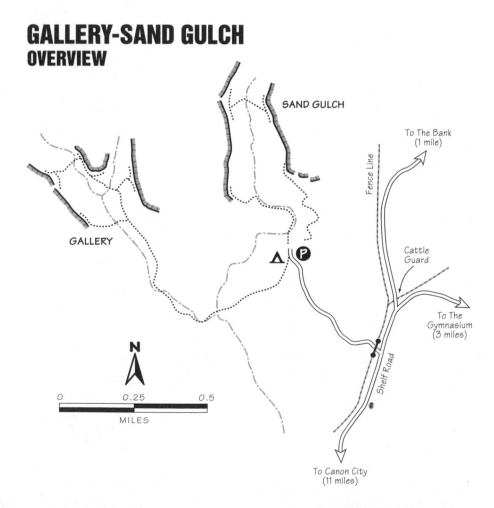

SAND GULCH

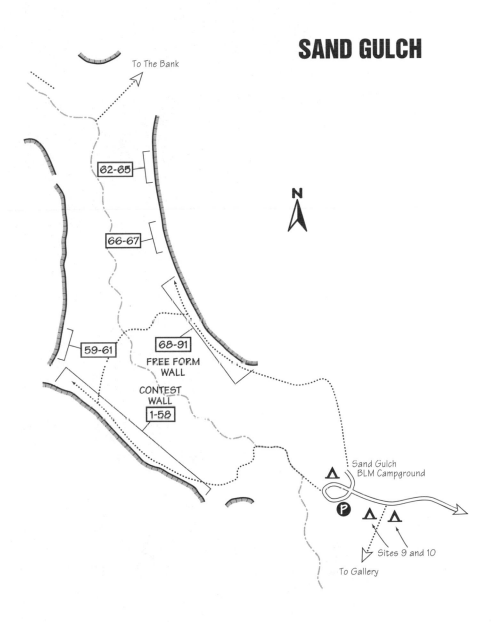

To The Bank

62-65

66-67

59-61

68-91
FREE FORM
WALL

CONTEST
WALL
1-58

N

Sand Gulch
BLM Campground

Sites 9 and 10

To Gallery

SAND GULCH OVERVIEW

Contest Wall
1 - 58

Freeform Wall
70-82

59-61

90-91

CONTEST WALL OVERVIEW

SAND GULCH
West Side

CONTEST WALL

1   Vail Athletic Club 5.11c (6c) ★

2   Dead Tree Crack 5.10b (6a) ★

3   Limestone Lady 5.11b/c (6c) ★

4   Scruples 5.11c/d (6c+) ★★
Continuous.

5   Slipper Queen 5.11d (7a) ★★
Devious.

6   Porkus Non Grata 5.10d/5.11a
(6b) ★★
Continuous.

7   Liquid Pork 5.11c (6c)

8   Dough Boys 5.10c/d (6b) ★
Cracks, use long runners.

CONTEST WALL

5   Slipper Queen 5.11d (7a) ★★
9   Unknown 5.11c (6c)
12 The Apple Bites Back 5.11c (6c) ★★★
17 The Armisist 5.10b (6a) ★
25 Spinney Dan 5.10c (6a+) ★★
28 Turbo Road 5.11d (7a) ★
33 Little Mecca 5.12a/b (7a+) ★★
37 Renaissance 5.11a (6b) ★

CONTEST WALL

1   *Vail Athletic Club 5.11c (6c)* ★
6   *Porkus Non Grata 5.10d/5.11a (6b)* ★★
12 *The Apple Bites Back 5.11c (6c)* ★★★
16 *Dune 5.10a (5+)* ★

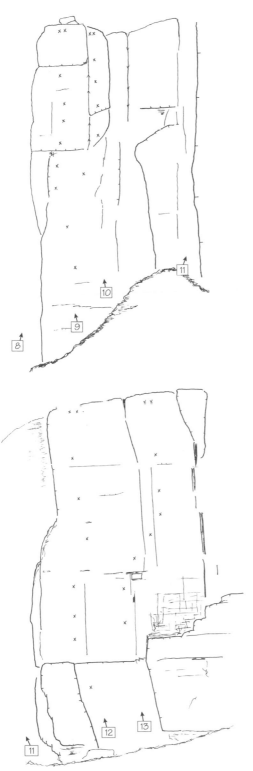

9 Unknown 5.11c (6c)

10 Jelly Bellies 5.10c (6a+) ★
Good position.

11 Not So Killer Bees 5.10d (6b) ★
Good rock, technical.

12 The Apple Bites Back 5.11c
(6c) ★★★
Great rock, thin.

13 Apple Jam Crack 5.11b (6c) ★
Cracks.

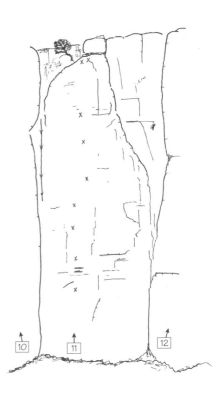

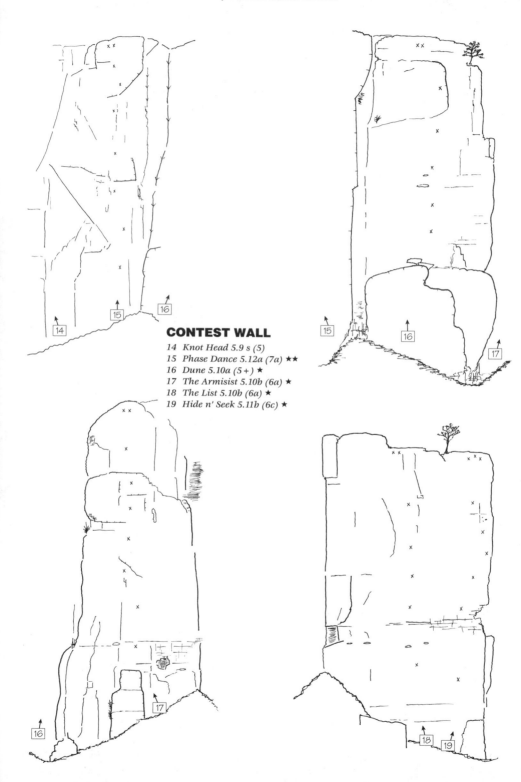

CONTEST WALL

14 *Knot Head 5.9 s (5)*
15 *Phase Dance 5.12a (7a)* ★★
16 *Dune 5.10a (5+)* ★
17 *The Armisist 5.10b (6a)* ★
18 *The List 5.10b (6a)* ★
19 *Hide n' Seek 5.11b (6c)* ★

CONTEST WALL

20 *Suburbia 5.10b/c (6a)* ★★★
22 *Metropolis 5.11d (7a)* ★★
25 *Spinney Dan 5.10c (6a+)* ★★
30 *Jump For Cholla 5.10d (6b)* ★
33 *Little Mecca 5.12a/b (7a+)* ★★
35 *Lime And Punishment 5.11b/c (6c)* ★★

continued on page 63

14 Knot Head 5.9 s (5)
Pro to 3".

15 Phase Dance 5.12a (7a) ★★
Strenuous, good position.

16 Dune 5.10a (5+) ★

17 The Armisist 5.10b (6a) ★

18 The List 5.10b (6a) ★

19 Hide n' Seek 5.11b (6c) ★

20 Suburbia 5.10b/c (6a) ★★★
Continuous, edges.

21 Book Of Bob 5.8 (5)
Pro to 5".

22 Metropolis 5.11d (7a) ★★
Difficult start, strenuous.

23 Miller Time 5.11a/b (6b+) ★★
Sequential, balance.

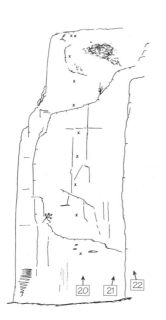

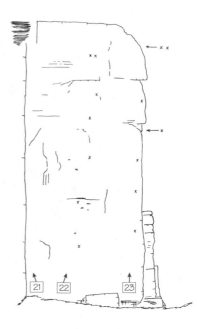

CONTEST WALL

20 *Suburbia 5.10b/c (6a)* ★★★
24 *Cactus Carrie 5.11b/c (6c)*
28 *Turbo Road 5.11d (7a)* ★

20

24

28

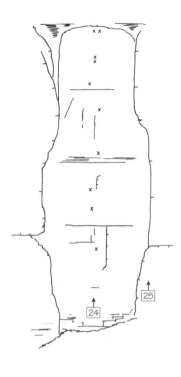

24 Cactus Carrie 5.11b/c (6c)
Continuous.

25 Spinney Dan 5.10c (6a+) ★★
Arête or face.

26 Hillbilly Bob 5.12a (7a) ★

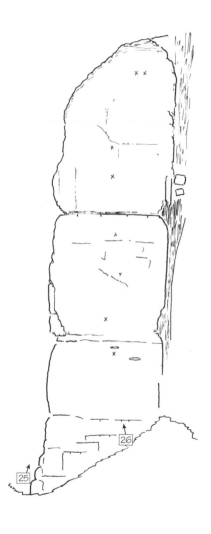

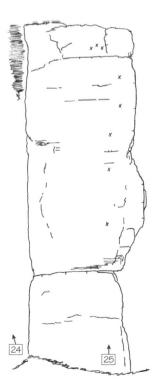

27 Bell Ringer 5.10b (6a)

28 Turbo Road 5.11d (7a) ★
   Sustained

29 Cattle Prod 5.11b/c (6c) ★

30 Jump For Cholla 5.10d (6b) ★

31 Don't Feed The Cholla 5.11b/c (6c)

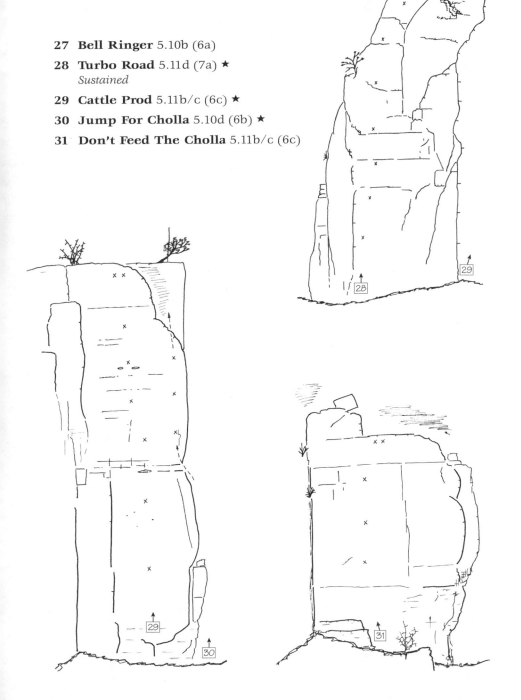

CONTEST WALL

28 *Turbo Road 5.11d (7a)* ★
34 *Cactus Drop 5.10d (6b)* ★★
39 *Limestone Politician 5.11b (6c)* ★
45 *Faris Of Horseman 5.12a (7a)* ★★
47 *Fossil Fueled 5.11a (6b)* ★

32 Trick or Treat 5.11b (6c) ★

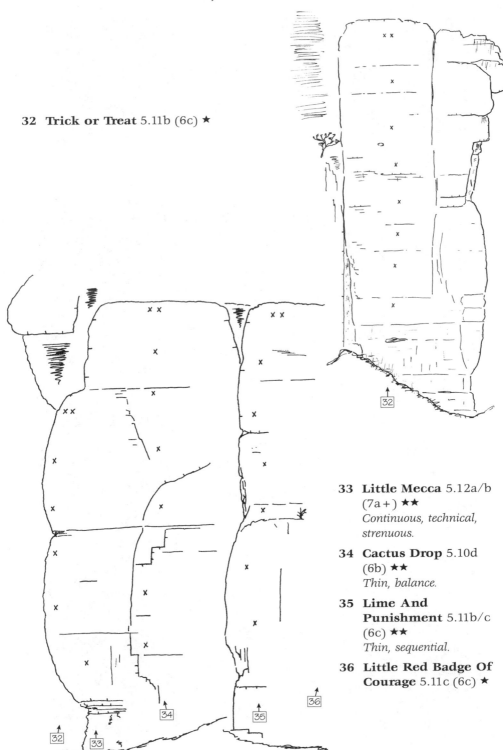

33 Little Mecca 5.12a/b
(7a+) ★★
*Continuous, technical,
strenuous.*

34 Cactus Drop 5.10d
(6b) ★★
Thin, balance.

**35 Lime And
Punishment** 5.11b/c
(6c) ★★
Thin, sequential.

**36 Little Red Badge Of
Courage** 5.11c (6c) ★

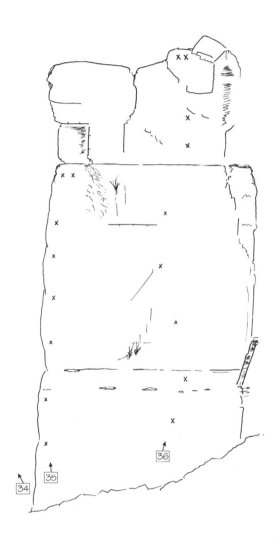

37 Renaissance 5.11a (6b) ★

38 Silverado 5.11b (6c) ★

39 Limestone Politician 5.11b (6c) ★

CONTEST WALL

40 *9 to 5 5.10d (6b)* ★★
43 *Rodao 5.11c (6c)* ★
45 *Farts Of Horseman 5.12a (7a)* ★★
47 *Fossil Fueled 5.11a (6b)* ★
49 *You Snooze, You Lose 5.11c/d (6c+)* ★★
57 *No Place For A Lady 5.12a (7a)* ★
59 *Arms Are For Hugging 5.11a (6b)*

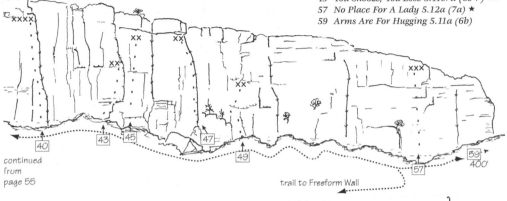

continued
from
page 55

trail to Freeform Wall

40 9 to 5 5.10d (6b) ★★

41 Short Slaughter 5.11a (6b) ★

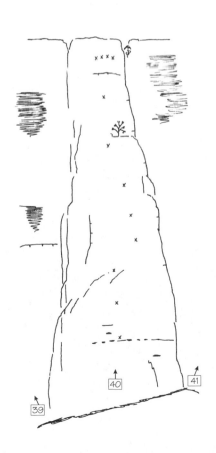

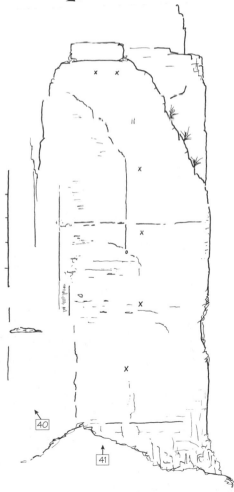

CONTEST WALL

43 *Rodeo 5.11c (6c)* ★
47 *Fossil Fueled 5.11a (6b)* ★
51 *Top Fun 5.10d (6b)*
57 *No Place For A Lady 5.12a (7a)* ★

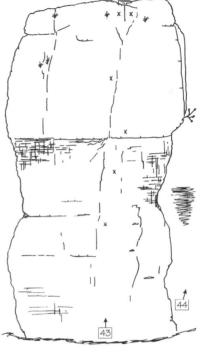

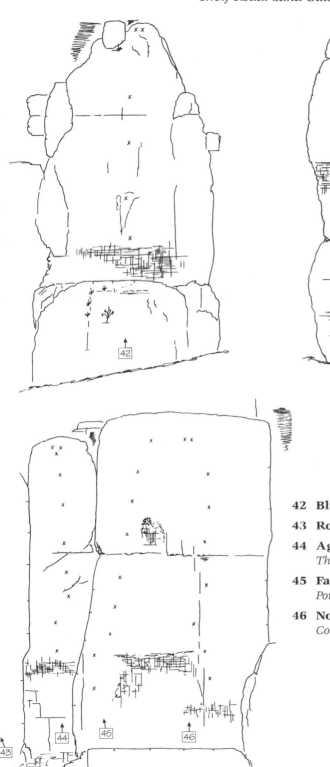

42 Blinky's Fun House 5.11b (6c) ★

43 Rodao 5.11c (6c) ★

44 Agent Orange 5.12a (7a) ★★
Thin.

45 Farts Of Horseman 5.12a (7a) ★★
Power moves.

46 No Tomorrow 5.12b (7b) ★★
Continuous, strenuous.

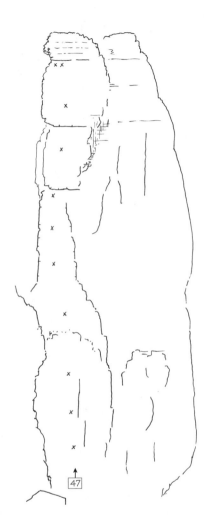

47 Fossil Fueled 5.11a (6b) ★

48 Monster Man 5.11d s (7a) ★
Strenuous.

49 You Snooze, You Lose 5.11c/d
(6c+) ★★
Strenuous, reaches.

50 Spice Is Nice 5.11d (7a) ★★
Strenuous.

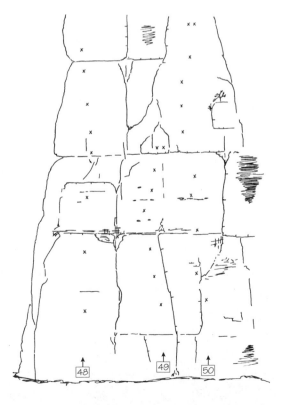

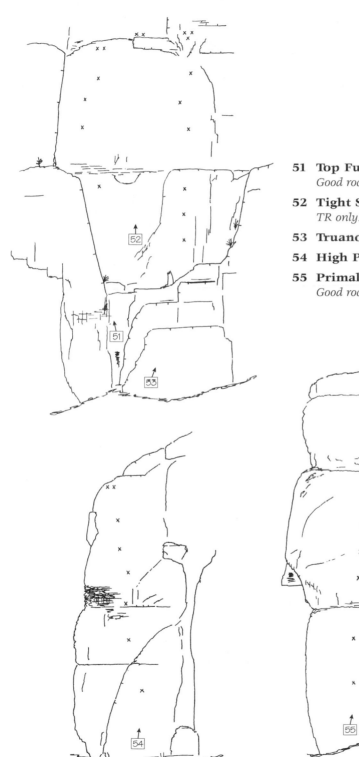

51 Top Fun 5.10d (6b)
Good rock, pockets.

52 Tight Squeeze 5.12b (7b)
TR only.

53 Truancy 5.11a (6b) ★

54 High Pocs 5.11c (6c)

55 Primal Urge 5.11c (6c) ★
Good rock, pockets.

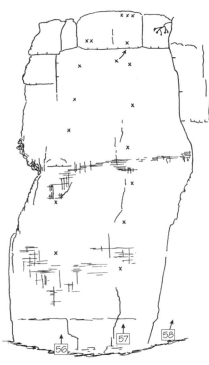

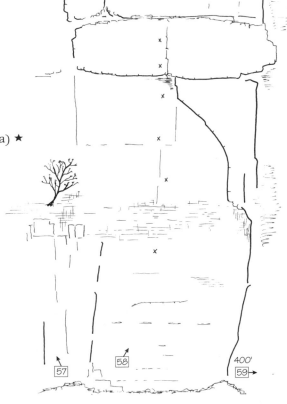

56 Unknown 5.11d/5.12a (7a) ★

57 No Place For A Lady 5.12a (7a) ★
Strenuous, roof.

58 Wasp 5.12a (7a) ★

59 Arms Are For Hugging 5.11a (6b)

60 Unknown 5.10d (6b) ★
Thin, very sharp.

61 Girls Night Out 5.10b (6a) ★
Very sharp.

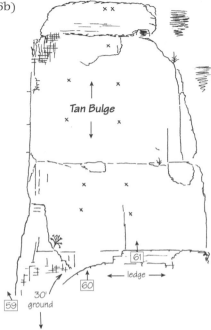

SAND GULCH
East Side

62 Infinite Dreams 5.11d (7a)

63 The Evil That Men Do 5.10c (6a+)

64 Operation Mind Crime 5.11d (7a)

65 Drunk Hicks With Guns 5.10c (6a+)

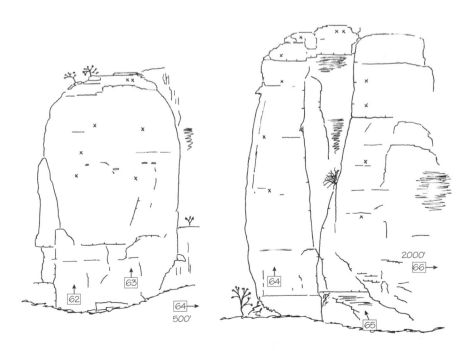

SAND GULCH—EAST SIDE

68 *Crystalized Water Vapor 5.10d (6b)* ★
70 *Habitat For Humanity 5.11a (6b)* ★
72 *Freeform 5.12a (7a)* ★★★

77 *Partners In Crime 5.11c/d (6c+)* ★★★
80 *Karma Mechanic 5.10a (5+)* ★★
84 *Berlin Wall 5.11a (6b)* ★
85 *Swinging Chimps 5.11a (6b)* ★

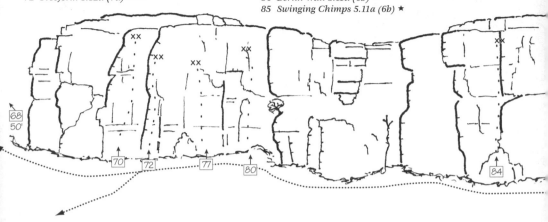

66 Dart 270 5.11b (6c)

67 Ma'at 5.11c/d (6c+)

68 Crystalized Water Vapor 5.10d (6b) ★

69 New World 5.10c (6a+) ★

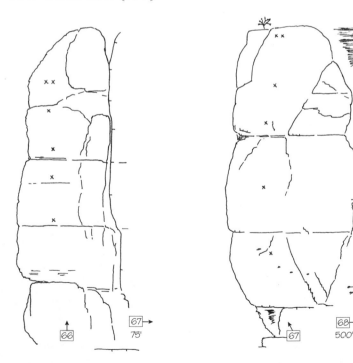

85 *Swinging Chimps 5.11a (6b)* ★
87 *Super Duper Crack 5.11b (6c)*
89 *Minimum Security 5.11c/d (6c+)* ★★★
90 *Red Rocket 5.12a (7a)* ★

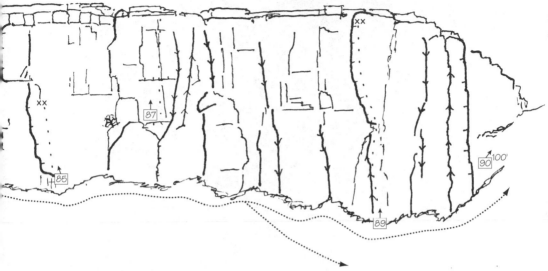

70 Habitat For Humanity 5.11a (6b) ★

71 Eddy D 5.10b (6a) ★

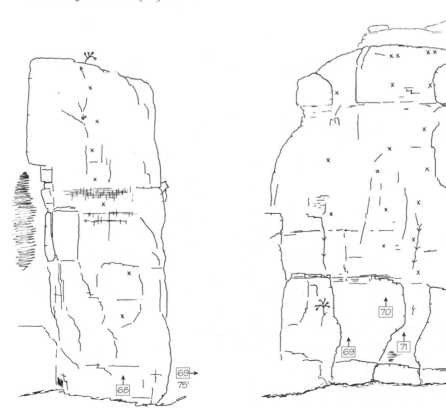

SAND GULCH—EAST SIDE

69 *New World 5.10c (6a+)* ★
72 *Freeform 5.12a (7a)* ★★★
79 *Village Idiot 5.11a (6b)* ★★
84 *Berlin Wall 5.11a (6b)* ★
86 *Onomatopoeia 5.12a (7a)* ★

72 Freeform 5.12a (7a) ★★★
Good position, strenuous, continuous.

73 Barney 5.9 (5)
Chimney.

74 Don't Think Twice 5.11b (6c) ★

75 Bad Brains 5.12a (7a) ★

76 Helter Skelter 5.11d (7a) ★★
Strenuous, continuous, reaches.

77 Partners In Crime 5.11c/d (6c+) ★★★
Reaches.

78 Cyborg 5.11b (6c) ★★
Strenuous.

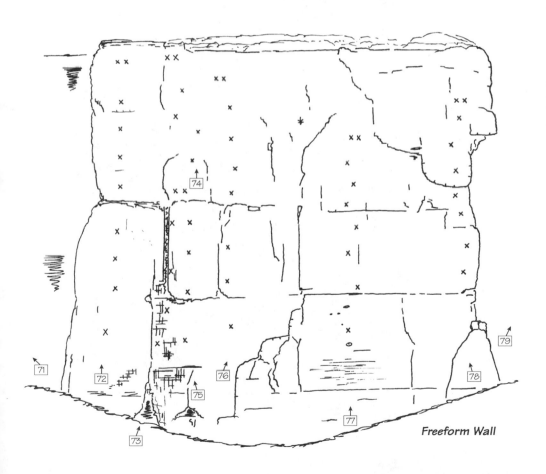

Freeform Wall

SAND GULCH - EAST SIDE

84 *Berlin Wall 5.11a (6b)* ★
85 *Swinging Chimps 5.11a (6b)* ★
87 *Super Duper Crack 5.11b (6c)*
89 *Minimum Security 5.11c/d (6c+)* ★★★

79 Village Idiot 5.11a (6b) ★★
Roof.

80 Karma Mechanic 5.10a
(5+) ★★
Continuous.

81 Bourgeois Belay Dogs 5.10b
(6a) ★

82 Helium Boys 5.11b (6c)

83 Guilty By Association 5.9+
(5+)
Two bolts.

84 Berlin Wall 5.11a (6b) ★

85 Swinging Chimps 5.11a (6b) ★

86 Onomatopoeia 5.12a (7a) ★

87 Super Duper Crack 5.11b (6c)
Pro to 3", roof to crack.

88 Nice Set Of Jugs 5.11a s (6b)
Two bolts.

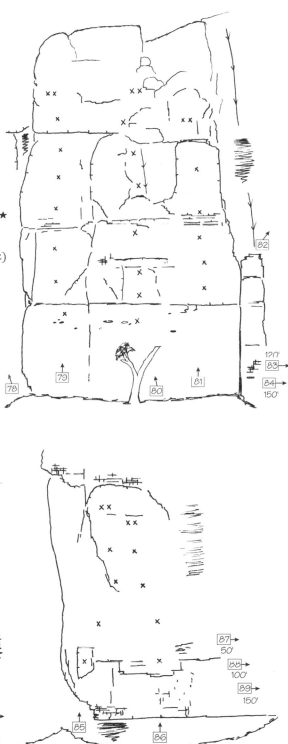

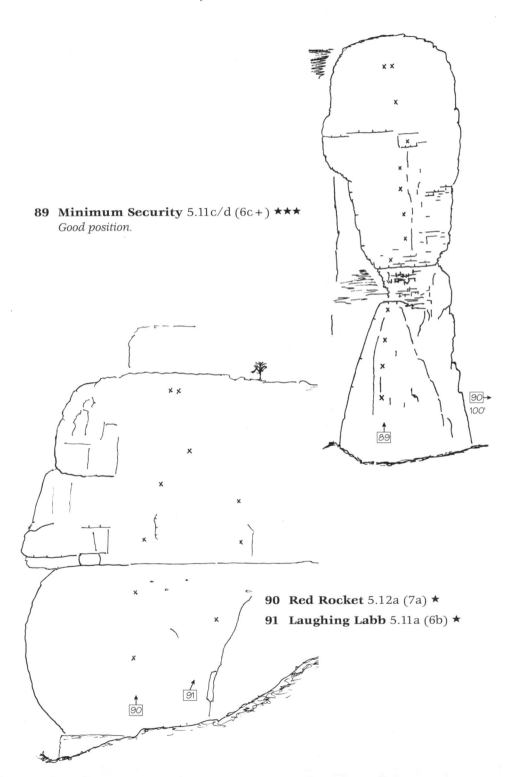

89 Minimum Security 5.11c/d (6c+) ★★★
Good position.

90 Red Rocket 5.12a (7a) ★
91 Laughing Labb 5.11a (6b) ★

Partners in Crime

DEAD COLT

Dead Colt is a widespread area with short climbs on good rock. All climbs face north and are better in the warmer summer months. With slightly less than a dozen routes, this small canyon is a seldom visited area.

From the parking areas at the stream crossing, climbs are located both upstream and downstream. See the overview map for trail locations. It is also possible to access Dead Colt from the (BLM) Bank Campground. Hike south-southwest into the streambed (Sand Gulch), and continue west; the climbs are located on the left (south). Approach time: 15 to 30 minutes.

DEAD COLT

DEAD COLT

5 Elvis Solution 5.11d (7a) ★
7 Air Conditioned Falls 5.11d (7a) ★

DEAD COLT
East

1   **Meaty, Beaty, Big and Bouncy** 5.12a (7a) ★

2   **Who's Next?** 5.11b/c (6c) ★

3   **Won't Get Fooled Again** 5.12a/b s (7a+)
    Cams from 1/2"–1".

4   **America Is Waiting** 5.11c (6c) ★

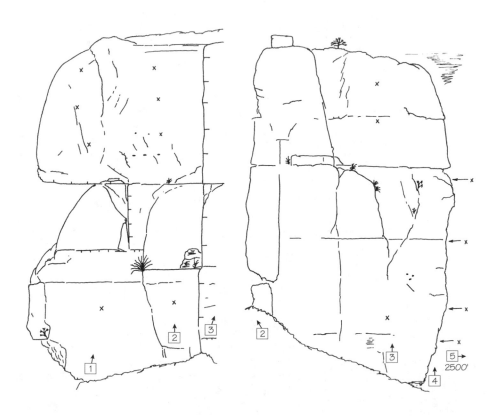

DEAD COLT
West

5   **Elvis Solution** 5.11d (7a) ★

6   **Infinite Rider On The Big
    Dogma** 5.12b (7b) ★
    Very thin.

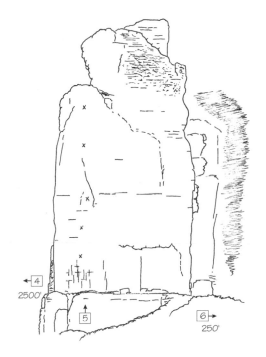

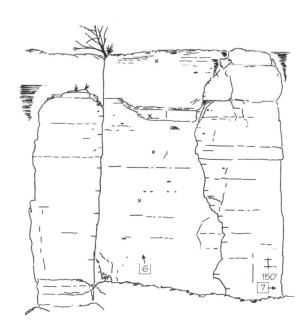

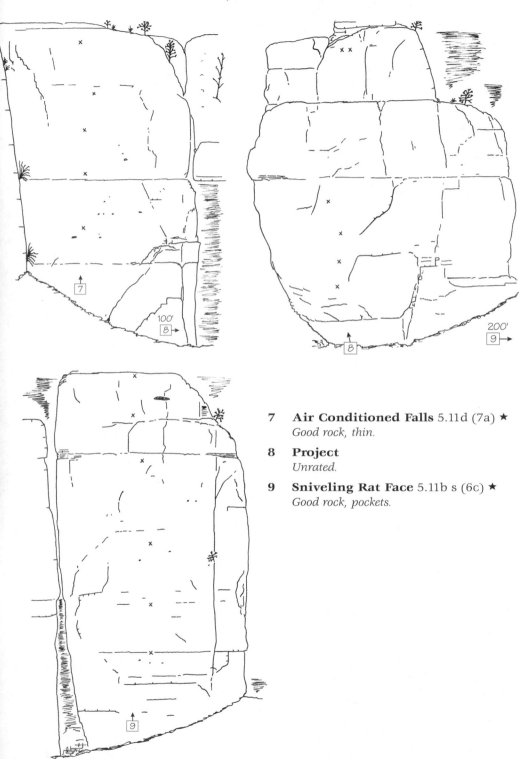

7   Air Conditioned Falls 5.11d (7a) ★
Good rock, thin.

8   Project
Unrated.

9   Sniveling Rat Face 5.11b s (6c) ★
Good rock, pockets.

Ric Geiman on "Staying Power"

BANK-DARK SIDE-CACTUS CLIFF-
SPINEY RIDGE-GYMNASIUM
OVERVIEW

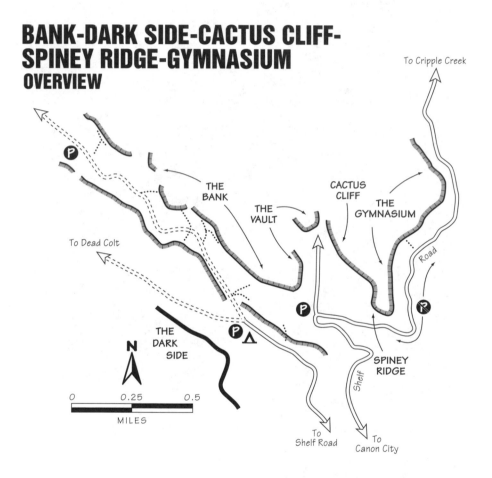

To Cripple Creek

THE
BANK

THE
VAULT

CACTUS
CLIFF

THE
GYMNASIUM

Road

To Dead Colt

THE
DARK
SIDE

N

SPINEY
RIDGE

Shelf

0   0.25   0.5

MILES

To
Shelf Road

To
Canon City

THE DARK SIDE

The Dark Side contains the most consistently good limestone at Shelf Road, usually black or grey and extensively pocketed. Climbs here tend to be in the upper range of difficulty, mostly 5.11 and above. For its entire length the cliff faces north, making this area a good summertime retreat from Shelf Road's blazing sun. By November the cliff tends to be cold, but warms up again by April.

The Dark Side may be approached in one of two different ways. From the Bank Campground, hike down the road into The Bank about 100 feet to the "2150 Wall" trailhead. Take this trail, which switchbacks east (marked by a sign) and eventually travels the base of The Dark Side. The other avenue of access is a gully near the eastern end of the cliff. East 300 feet from the Bank Campground is a pullout marked for group camping; this is directly on top of the Dark Side. Follow a trail along the top of the cliff 0.25 mile east until cairns mark a descent gully. A fixed rope helps to make the descent third class. Approach time: 10-20 minutes.

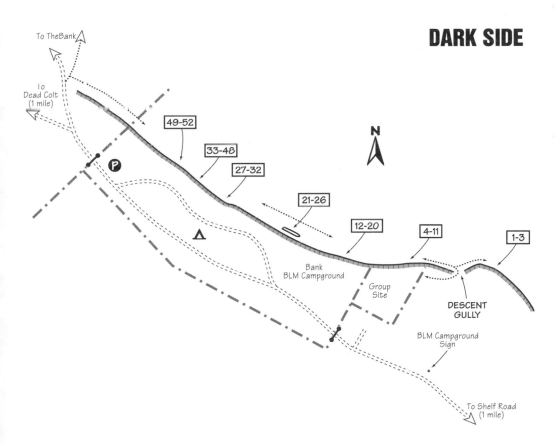

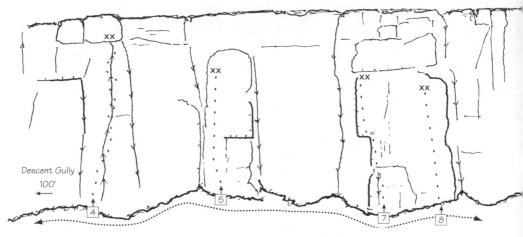

THE DARK SIDE

1   Slide It In 5.12b/c (7b) ★
Thin.

2   Stuck In The Middle With You 5.11b/c (6c) ★

3   Papillon 5.12a (7a) ★
Sharp, squeezed.

THE DARK SIDE

4   *Slap Me 5.11d (7a)* ★
5   *Levels Of The Game 5.12a (7a)*
7   *Whisper To A Scream 5.11d (7a)* ★★
8   *Black' n' Dicey 5.10a (5+)* ★★

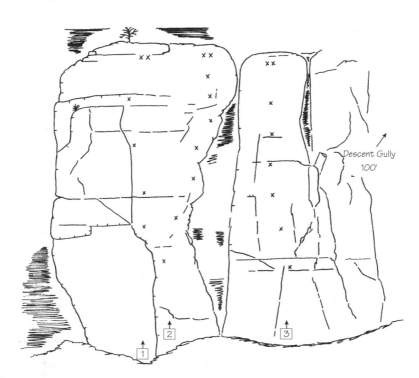

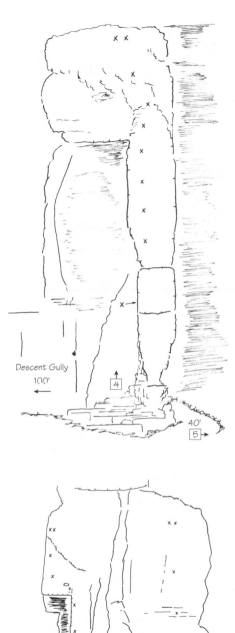

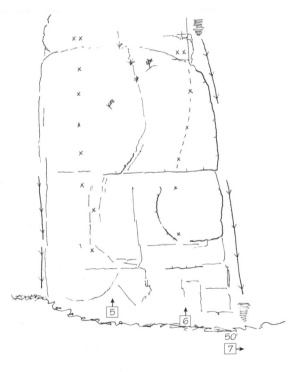

4 Slap Me 5.11d (7a) ★

5 Levels Of The Game 5.12a (7a) ★
Devious.

6 Unknown 5.11b/c (6c)

7 Whisper To A Scream 5.11d (7a) ★★
Good position, sequential.

8 Black' n' Dicey 5.10a (5+) ★★
Great rock, balance.

THE DARK SIDE

2   *Stuck In The Middle With You 5.11b/c (6c)* ★
7   *Whisper To A Scream 5.11d (7a)* ★★
11   *Red Lined 5.11b (6c)* ★★

THE DARK SIDE

7 *Whisper To A Scream 5.11d (7a)* ★★
11 *Red Lined 5.11b (6c)* ★★
14 *Bax Lunch 5.11a/b (6b+)* ★★★
25 *The Cracks On Top 5.11a/b (6b+)* ★★
27 *Suspender Man 5.11d (7a)* ★★

The Bank
Campground

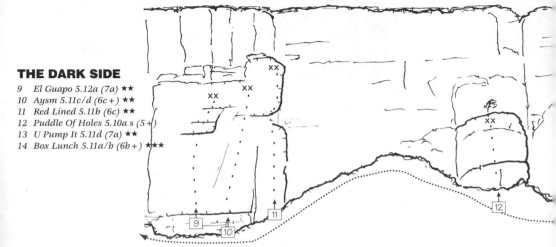

THE DARK SIDE

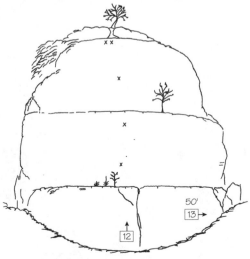

9   El Guapo 5.12a (7a) ★★
Thin, strenuous.

10   Aysm 5.11c/d (6c+) ★★

11   Red Lined 5.11b (6c) ★★

12   Puddle Of Holes 5.10a s (5+)
Great rock, pockets.

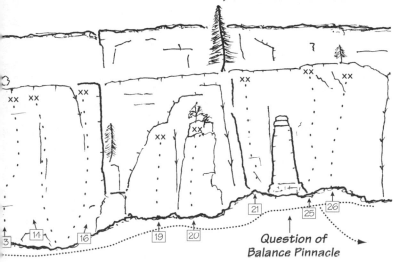

Question of
Balance Pinnacle

THE DARK SIDE

16 *Yauza 5.12a (7a)* ★★
19 *Kinesthesia 5.12a (7a)* ★
20 *Punjabi 5.11a/b (6b+)* ★★
21 *Enchanted Porkfist 5.11a (6b)* ★★★
25 *The Cracks On Top 5.11a/b (6b+)* ★★
26 *Muted By Reality 5.11a/b (6b+)* ★★

13 U Pump It 5.11d (7a) ★★
Continuous

14 Box Lunch 5.11a/b (6b+) ★★★
Good rock, continuous.

15 Eat, Drink and Beat Larry 5.12b
(7b) ★★
Technical, thin.

16 Yauza 5.12a (7a) ★★
Thin face to crack.

17 Kashmere 5.12c-5.13b
(7b+/8a) ★★★
*Perfect rock, prow, pockets, technical;
height dependent.*

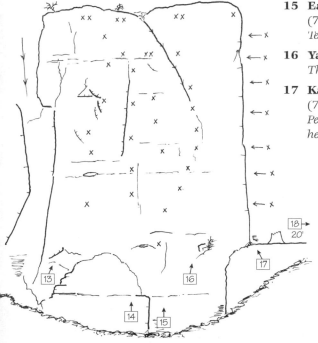

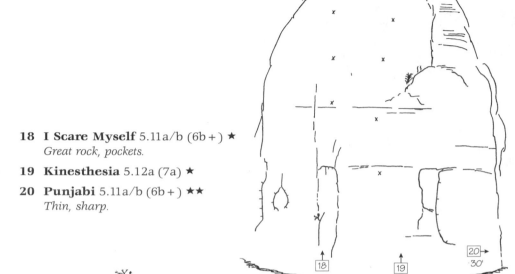

18 I Scare Myself 5.11a/b (6b+) ★
Great rock, pockets.

19 Kinesthesia 5.12a (7a) ★

20 Punjabi 5.11a/b (6b+) ★★
Thin, sharp.

21 Enchanted Porkfist 5.11a (6b) ★★★
Great rock, continuous.

22 Lumina 5.9 (5) ★★★
Good rock, pockets, cracks.

QUESTION OF BALANCE PINNACLE

23 Fragile 5.10c (6a+) ★

24 Counter Balance 5.10c (6a+) ★

THE DARK SIDE

25 The Cracks On Top 5.11a/b (6b+) ★★

26 Muted By Reality 5.11a/b (6b+) ★★

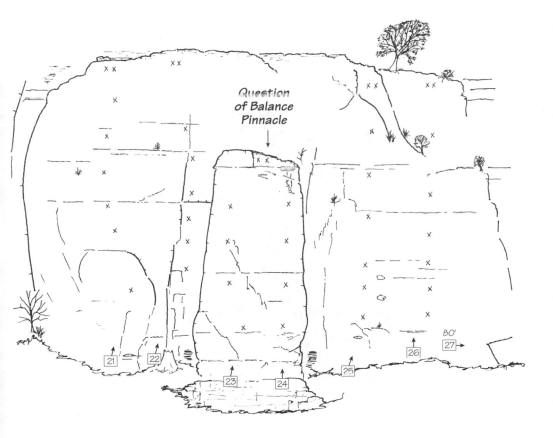

THE DARK SIDE

27　*Suspender Man 5.11d (7a)* ★★
34　*Void Lloyd 5.12a (7a)* ★★
39　*Call From Overseas 5.12a (7a)* ★★
43　*The Audition 5.12b/c (7b)* ★★★
47　*Two Hearts 5.11b/c (6c)* ★★★

THE DARK SIDE

31 *Corner Pockets 5.10c s (6a+)* ★
34 *Void Lloyd 5.12a (7a)* ★★
36 *The Welcoming 5.11c (6c)* ★
39 *Call From Overseas 5.12a (7a)* ★★

43 *The Audition 5.12b/c (7b)* ★★★
46 *Line Of Strength 5.12c s (7b+)* ★★★
47 *Two Hearts 5.11b/c (6c)* ★★★
49 *Edge O' Fright 5.10b/c (6a)* ★

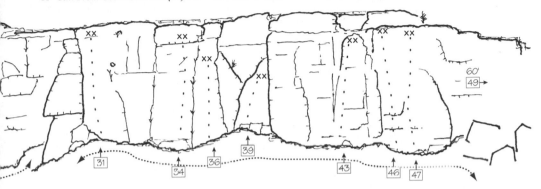

27 Suspender Man 5.11d (7a) ★★
Thin to large holds.

28 Unknown 5.10b (6a)
No hangers.

29 Thank Heaven For Little Girls 5.10d (6b) ★★
Great rock.

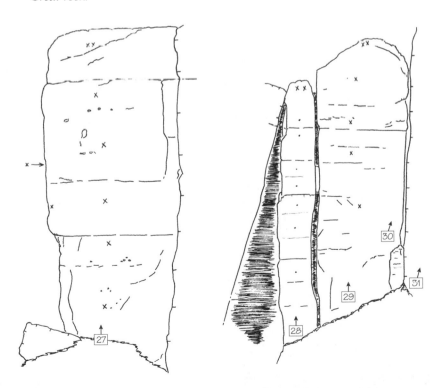

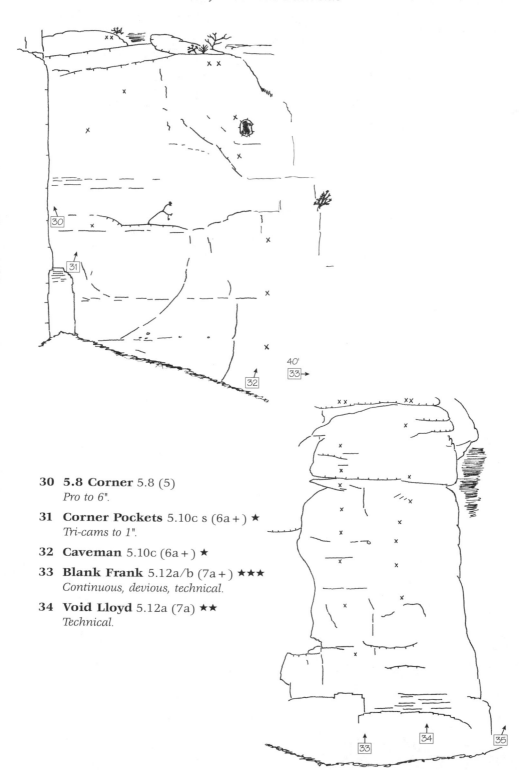

30 5.8 Corner 5.8 (5)
Pro to 6".

31 Corner Pockets 5.10c s (6a+) ★
Tri-cams to 1".

32 Caveman 5.10c (6a+) ★

33 Blank Frank 5.12a/b (7a+) ★★★
Continuous, devious, technical.

34 Void Lloyd 5.12a (7a) ★★
Technical.

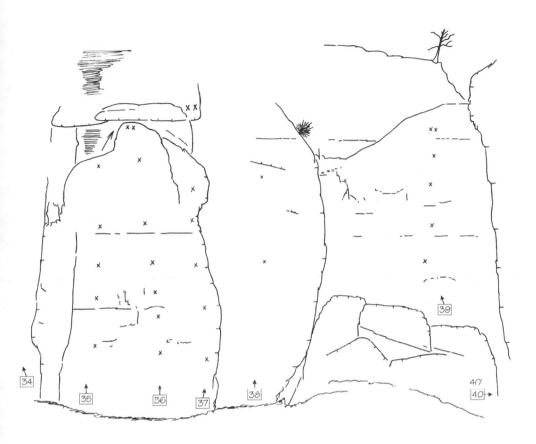

35 Go East Old Man 5.12a (7a) ★
Strenuous.

36 The Welcoming 5.11c (6c) ★

37 Trolling For Holds 5.10c (6a+)

38 Project 5.13c (8a+)

39 Call From Overseas 5.12a (7a) ★★
Perfect rock, technical, balance.

40 Unknown 5.10a (5+)

41 Black Awareness 5.11b (6c) ★★
Great rock, sequential.

42 Cracks Happen 5.11b (6c) ★★
Thin cracks.

43 The Audition 5.12b/c (7b) ★★★
Great rock, technical, continuous.

44 Mannequin 5.12c (7b+) ★
Great rock, very thin.

45 Unknown 5.11b/c (6c)
Cracks.

46 Line Of Strength 5.12c s
(7b+) ★★★
*Very continuous, strenuous, pre-clip first
bolt.*

47 Two Hearts 5.11b/c (6c) ★★★
Bulge, roof, cracks, face.

48 The Eagle Has Landed 5.12c-
5.13a (7b+ to 7c+) ★★
*Height dependent, bulging, very thin,
reaches.*

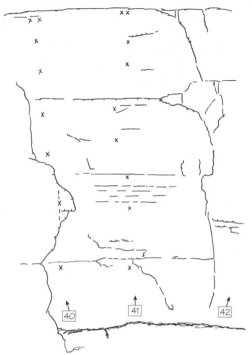

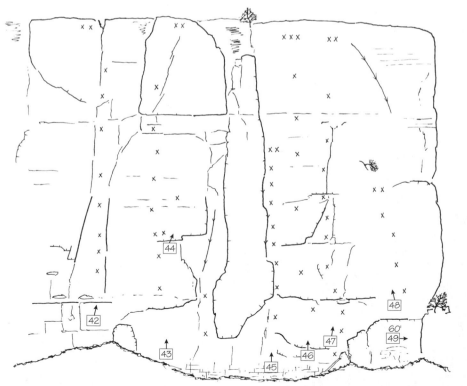

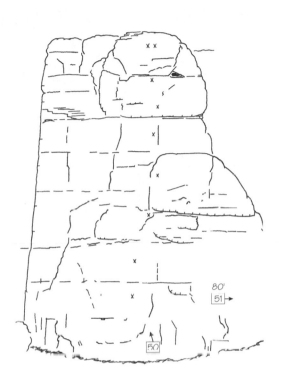

49 Edge O' Fright 5.10b/c (6a) ★
Arête.

50 The Swinging Richards 5.12b
(7b) ★★
Thin, sharp, roof.

51 Bonnie 5.10d (6b)

52 Clyde 5.11a (6b)

THE BANK

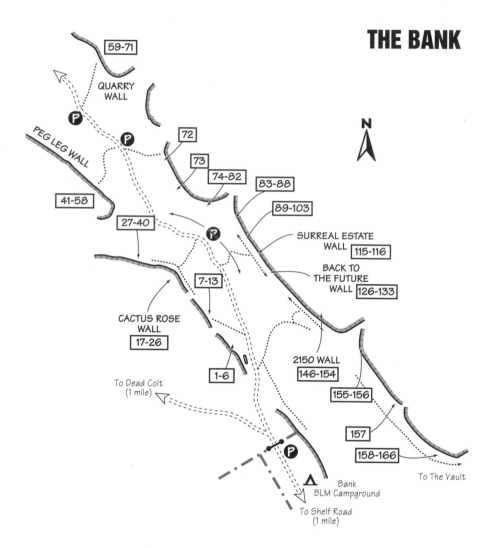

59-71

QUARRY
WALL

PEG LEG WALL

N

72

73

74-82

83-88

89-103

41-58

27-40

SURREAL ESTATE
WALL 115-116

BACK TO
THE FUTURE
WALL 126-133

7-13

CACTUS ROSE
WALL

17-26

2150 WALL
146-154

1-6

155-156

To Dead Colt
(1 mile)

157

158-166

To The Vault

Bank
BLM Campground

To Shelf Road
(1 mile)

THE BANK

The Bank was the first area developed on BLM land and has the largest concentration of climbs at Shelf Road. In addition, this area contains a large variety of limestone types, from white and tan sandstone-like rock to black and grey pocketed rock. The climbs in The Bank have a large range of difficulty, from 5.9 up to 5.13, while the majority are in the 5.11 category. The Bank is also a large area, stretching well over a mile, with cliffs facing in all directions.

A road travels through The Bank, with trails departing from several points. Note that this one-mile section of road is closed to parking. Small signs are in place at some of the trailheads, while others are marked only by cairns. For some reason, the signs along the road are frequently missing. Check the overview map for trail locations. Approach time: 5-15 minutes.

Kristine Thompson on Hostile Crankover
5.11c (6c).

THE BANK
South Side

1   **The Tower Of Beta** 5.12b (7b) ★

2   **Back In Black** 5.10d (6b)

3   **Child's Play** 5.12a (7a)

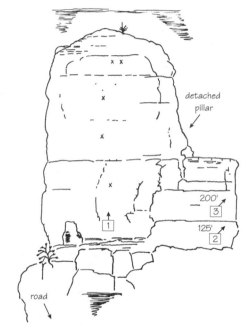

4   **The Omen** 5.10d (6b) ★

5   **Apollyon** 5.9 (5)
    Pro to 2 1/2".

6   **Sherpa Chicks** 5.11b (6c)

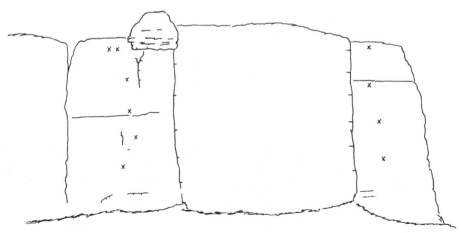

Preston Hopfenspringer on McFly 5.12d (7c).

THE BANK

7   *Raising Arizona 5.10d (6b)* ★
10 *Please Send Advil 5.12c (7b+)* ★★
12 *Desert Rose 5.11a (6b+)* ★
13 *Paradise Lost 5.12b/c s (7b)* ★

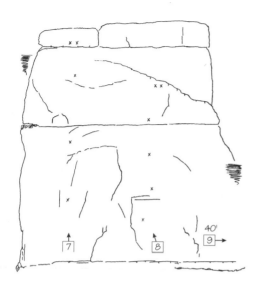

7   Raising Arizona 5.10d (6b) ★
Reaches.

8   Arizona Rising 5.11a (6b) ★
Good rock.

9   Le Menestrel Cycle 5.12c s
(7b+) ★★
Thin, reaches.

10 Please Send Advil 5.12c
(7b+) ★★
Very thin, tendon injury potential.

11 Driven To Tears 5.12a/b
(7a+) ★
Sharp.

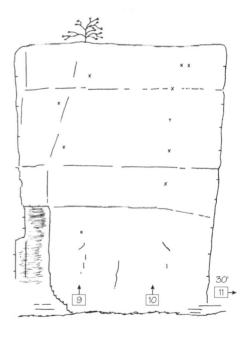

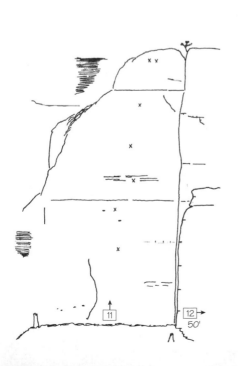

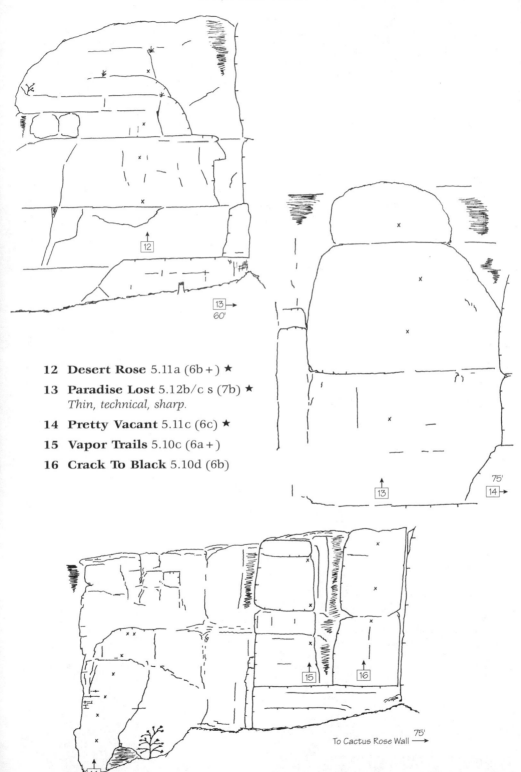

12   **Desert Rose** 5.11a (6b+) ★

13   **Paradise Lost** 5.12b/c s (7b) ★
Thin, technical, sharp.

14   **Pretty Vacant** 5.11c (6c) ★

15   **Vapor Trails** 5.10c (6a+)

16   **Crack To Black** 5.10d (6b)

To Cactus Rose Wall ⟶

THE BANK

14 *Pretty Vacant 5.11c (6c)* ★
16 *Crack To Black 5.10d (6b)*

CACTUS ROSE WALL (ROUTES 17-26)

17 *Welcome To The Machine 5.11d (7a)* ★★
21 *John Wayne Never Wore Boxer Shorts 5.10d (6L)*
25 *Cactus Rose 5.11d s (7a)* ★

CACTUS ROSE WALL (ROUTES 17-26)

17 Welcome To The Machine 5.11d (7a) ★★
Thin, continuous.

18 Mark Finds Bob Bolting 5.10d (6b) ★

19 Sweat Hog 5.10d (6b)

20 The Needle Lies 5.10a/b (6a) ★

21 John Wayne Never Wore Boxer Shorts 5.10d (6b)

22 Bacher Against The Wall And Kauk Her 5.11a/b (6b+) ★

23 Sticks and Stones May Break My Bones, But Whips and Chains Excite Me 5.9+ (5+) ★
Pro to 3 1/2".

24 E = mc2 5.11c/d (6c+) ★★
Reaches.

25 Cactus Rose 5.11d s (7a) ★

26 Barbecuing Traditions 5.12b (7b) ★★
Pockets, strenuous.

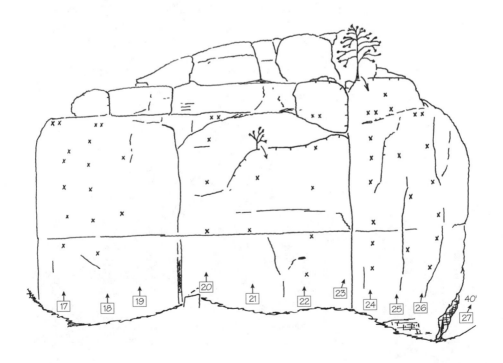

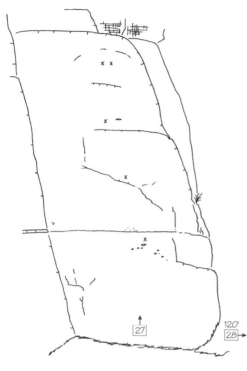

27 **Feathers Edge** 5.12a (7a)
Devious.

28 **Maidens Milk** 5.10c (6a +)

29 **Dancing Digits** 5.12a (7a)

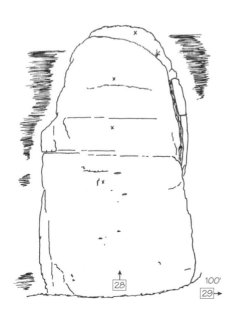

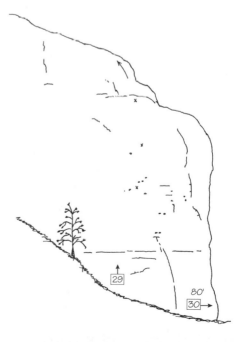

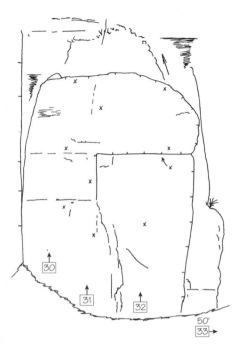

30 Aliens Ate My Penis 5.11b/c (6c)
Sustained.

31 Paper Bondage 5.10a (5 +)

32 Handsome Alien 5.12a (7a) ★

33 Munchkins On Parade 5.10c
(6a +)

34 Ultimatum 5.12c/d (7c) ★
Thin, technical, tendon injury potential.

35 Skinheads Big Night Out 5.11d
(7a) ★
Strenuous, sequential.

**36 Take The Skinheads
Bowling** 5.11b (6c) ★
Strenuous.

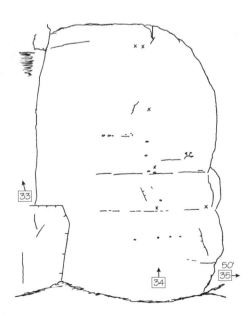

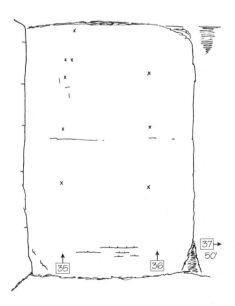

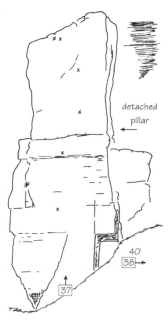

detached
pillar
←

37 Canada Cooler 5.12c (7b +) ★
Strenuous.

38 Little Boy With The Little Toy 5.10a (5 +)

39 Hell Razors 5.10b (6a)

40 Bondage Pig 5.9 (5)

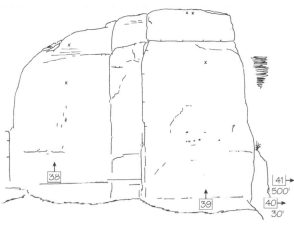

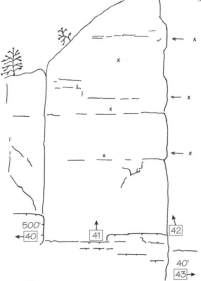

41 Fly Little Super Boy 5.11d (7a)

42 Arête Verde 5.11b (6c) ★

43 Close To The Bone 5.11d (7a)

44 Men Of Iron 5.9+ (5+)

**45 The Flamed, The Pumped,
The French** 5.11a (6b)
Good protection, strenuous.

46 Promised Land 5.11b/c (6c) ★

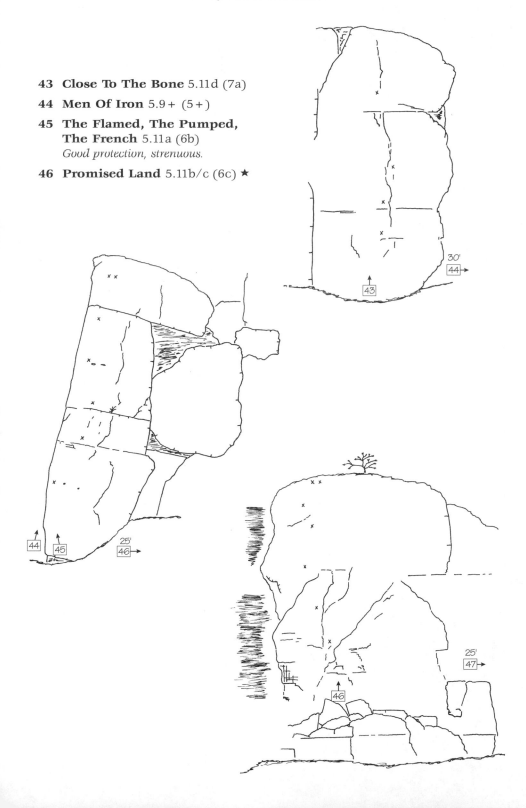

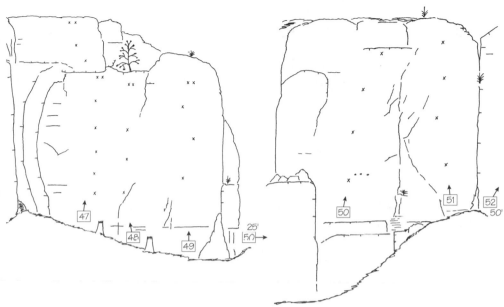

47 Clutching At Straws 5.11b &
5.12b/c (6c & 7b) ★★
Two pitches; devious, technical.

48 Catch The Wave 5.11c/d (6c+) ★

49 Surf's Up 5.11d (7a) ★

50 Sex Wax 5.11a (6b)

51 Best For Your Stick 5.10c (6a+)

52 Dog On It 5.11a s (6b)
Good rock, pockets.

53 Chili Dog 5.11a (6b)
Good rock.

54 Corn Dog 5.10c (6a+)

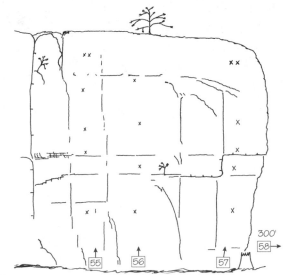

PEG LEG WALL
(ROUTES 55-57)

55 Part Insect 5.12b (7b) ★
Good rock, technical.

56 Mr. Peg Leg Speedwork 5.12a
    (7a) ★
Good rock, strenuous.

57 Adversary 5.12d (7c) ★

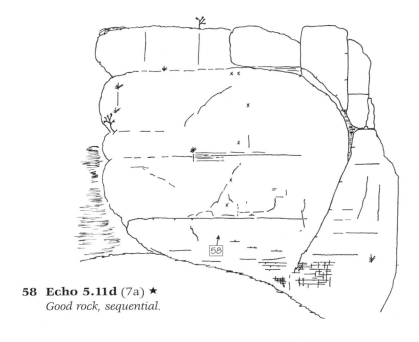

58 Echo 5.11d (7a) ★
Good rock, sequential.

Mark Van Horn footloose on the roof of Dave Dangle 5.11b/c (6c).

THE BANK - NORTH SIDE

59 *Anarchy X 5.11a/b (6b+)*
62 *Stone Cold Bush 5.11c (6c)* ★
64 *Bambi Meets Gdzilla 5.10c (6a+)* ★★

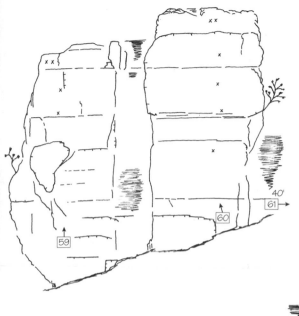

THE BANK
North Side

59 Anarchy X 5.11a/b (6b+)
Pro to 3".

60 Impending Doom 5.10c/d (6b)

61 Crack Night 5.11b/c (6c)

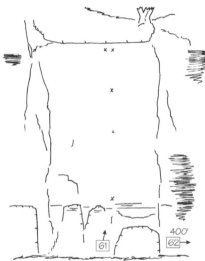

62 Stone Cold Bush 5.11c (6c) ★

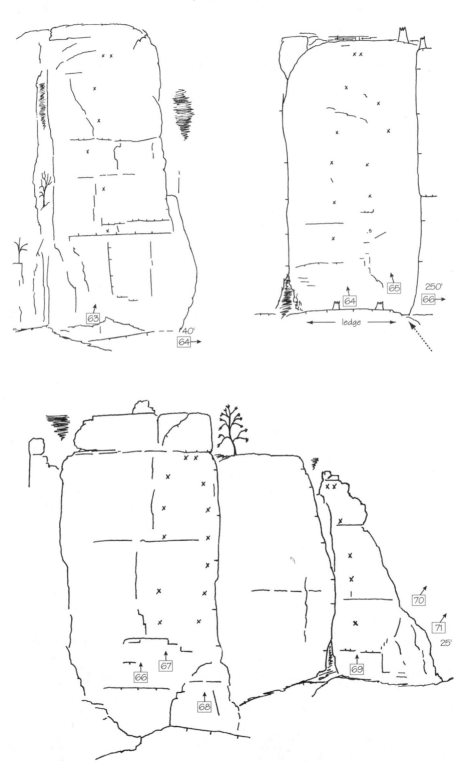

63 First Incisions 5.11b/c (6c) ★
Roofs, strenuous.

64 Bambi Meets Godzilla 5.10c (6a+) ★★
Continuous.

65 Tendon Respite 5.10a (5+) ★

66 Cold Finger 5.9+ s (5+)
Pro to 3".

67 Alfalfa Omega 5.10b (6a) ★

68 Dust Lust 5.10d (6b) ★★
Good position.

69 A Sharp 5.10b (6a) ★

70 Woodwind 5.9 s (5)
Pro to 5".

71 Bits and Pieces 5.10b (6a) ★

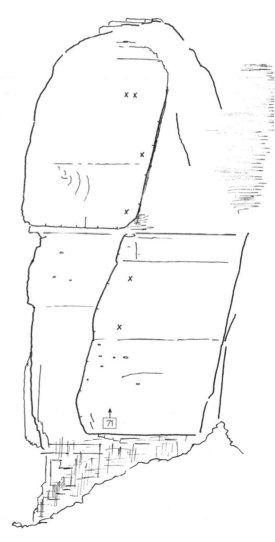

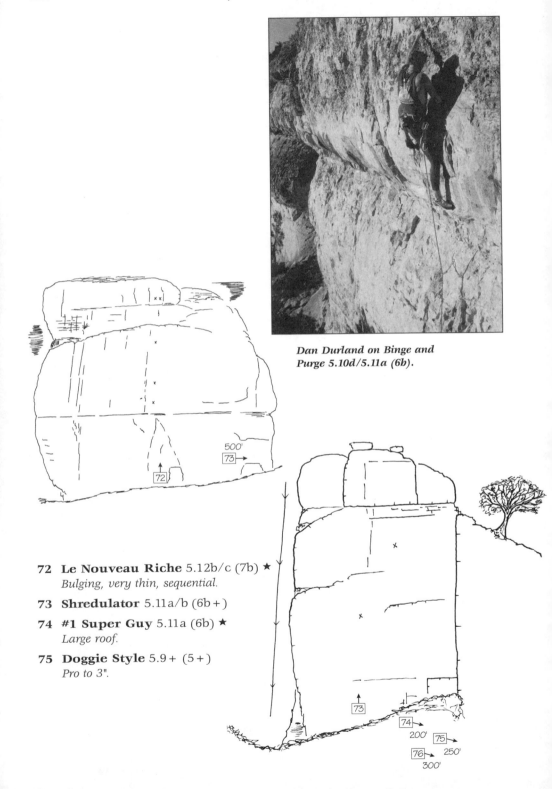

Dan Durland on Binge and Purge 5.10d/5.11a (6b).

72 Le Nouveau Riche 5.12b/c (7b) ★
Bulging, very thin, sequential.

73 Shredulator 5.11a/b (6b+)

74 #1 Super Guy 5.11a (6b) ★
Large roof.

75 Doggie Style 5.9+ (5+)
Pro to 3".

THE BANK - NORTH SIDE

72 *Le Nouveau Riche 5.12b/c (7b)* ★
73 *Shredulator 5.11a/b (6b+)*

THE BANK - NORTH SIDE

74 #1 Super Guy 5.11a (6b) ★
77 Puking Yuppies 5.11a s (6b)
80 Flesh Tuxedo 5.11b s (6c) ★★

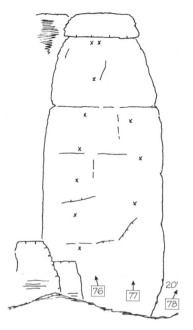

76 Starving Hippies 5.11b/c (6c) ★★
Continuous, sharp.

77 Puking Yuppies 5.11a s (6b)
Pro to 1 1/2".

78 Incredible Weather 5.12c/d (7c) ★★

79 The Flushings 5.10d vs (6b)
Pro to 2".

80 Flesh Tuxedo 5.11b s (6c) ★★
Poor rock.

81 The Sweepings 5.10a (5+)
Squeezed.

82 The Apple Cracks 5.9 s (5)
Pro to 5".

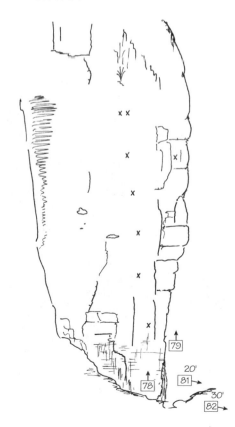

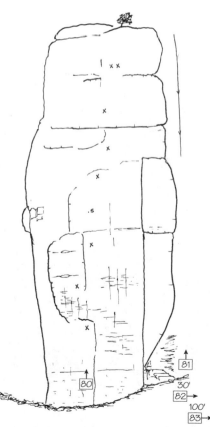

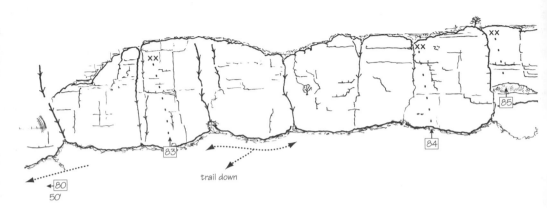

THE BANK — NORTH SIDE
83 *Richter Scale 5.10c (6a+)* ★★
84 *On The Mushroom 5.11b (6c)* ★
85 *Neapolitan Headrush 5.12a (7a)* ★

THE BANK — NORTH SIDE
83 *Richter Scale 5.10c (6a+)* ★★
84 *On The Mushroom 5.11b (6c)* ★
86 *Walking On The Moon 5.12c-5.13a/b (7b+ to 8a)* ★
90 *OI! 5.11a (6b)*

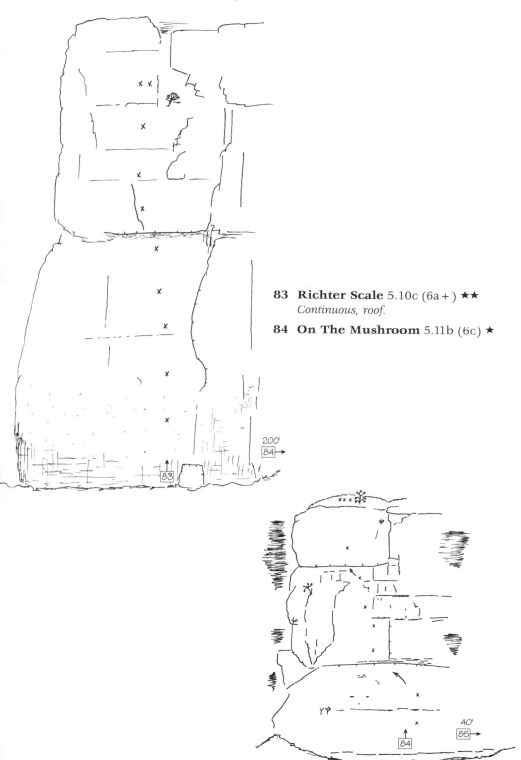

83 Richter Scale 5.10c (6a+) ★★
Continuous, roof.

84 On The Mushroom 5.11b (6c) ★

85 Neapolitan Headrush 5.12a (7a) ★

86 Walking On The Moon 5.12c-5.13a/b (7b+ to 8a) ★
Height-dependent, power moves.

87 Project 5.13b/c (8a)

88 On The Ritz 5.11b (6c) ★

89 Crow King 5.11c (6c) ★

90 OI! 5.11a (6b)

91 Energizer 5.12a (7a)

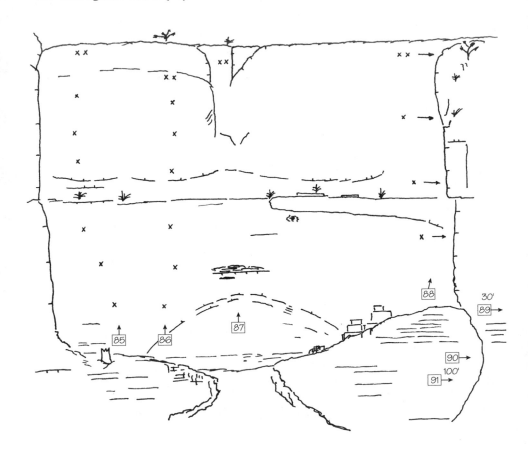

THE BANK - NORTH SIDE

90 Oi! 5.11a (6b)
95 Dave Dangle 5.11b/c (6c) ★★
97 Scarf and Barf 5.11b/c (6c) ★
100 Hostile Crankover 5.11c (6c) ★★
103 War In The Banks 5.10b (6a) ★★
107 Thunder Tactics 5.11c/d (6c+) ★★★★

THE BANK – NORTH SIDE

89 *Crow King 5.11c (6c)* ★
95 *Dave Dangle 5.11b/c (6c)* ★★

98 *Binge and Purge 5.10d/5.11a (6b)* ★★
100 *Hostile Crankover 5.11c (6c)* ★★
103 *War In The Banks 5.10b (6a)* ★

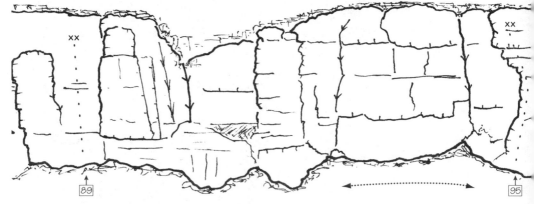

92 On Crack 5.10c vs (6a+)
Pro to 3".

93 Off Crack 5.10d vs (6b)
Pro to 6".

94 Power Broker 5.12c/d (7c) ★★
Power moves, roofs.

95 Dave Dangle 5.11b/c (6c) ★★
Roofs.

96 Team Anorexia 5.10d/5.11a (6b)

97 Scarf and Barf 5.11b/c (6c) ★
Thin.

98 Binge and Purge 5.10d/5.11a
(6b) ★★

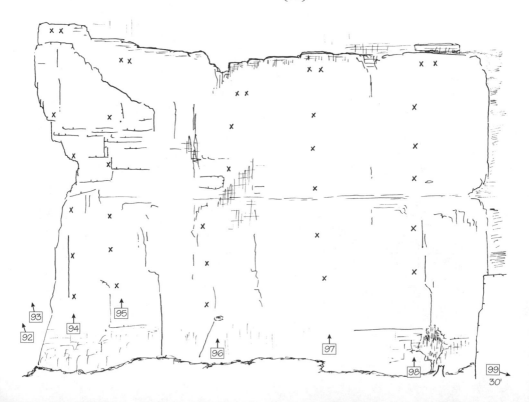

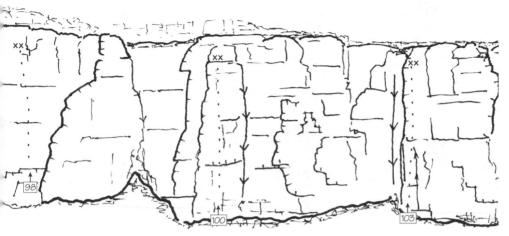

99   **Aspiring Frog** 5.10c/d (6b) ★

100 **Hostile Crankover** 5.11c (6c) ★★
Roof to face.

101 **Energy Before Ecstacy** 5.10a/b (6a)

102 **Shy Roof** 5.11b (6c)
Pro to 3 1/2", large roof.

103 **War In The Banks** 5.10b (6a) ★
Good rock, devious.

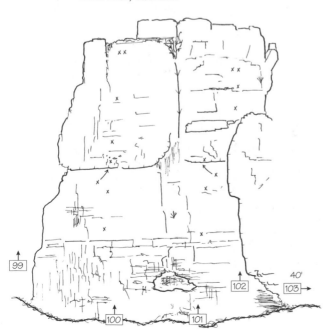

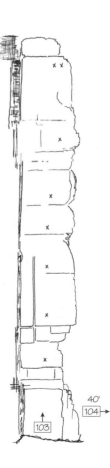

THE BANK – NORTH SIDE

103 *War In The Banks 5.10b (6a)* ★
108 *Otis 5.12b/c (7b)*
113 *Sparkle In The Rain 5.12c (7b+)* ★★★

SURREAL ESTATE WALL

116 *Heavy Weather 5.12a/b (7a+)* ★★★
119 *Ice Cream Hangover 5.11b/c (6c)* ★★★

BACK TO THE FUTURE WALL

129 *No Rest For The Wicked 5.12a (7a)* ★
135 *BC 5.9+ (5+)* ★

104 Tsunami 5.9+ (5+)
Pro to 2".

105 Thunder Thighs 5.11a/b (6b+) ★

106 Dr. Zeus 5.12b/c (7b) ★

107 Thunder Tactics 5.11c/d (6c+) ★★★
Bulging, sequential.

108 Otis 5.12b/c (7b)
Power moves.

109 Project
Unrated.

110 Project 5.13b/c (8a)

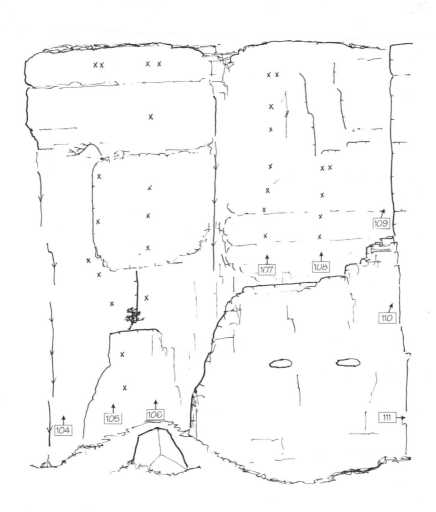

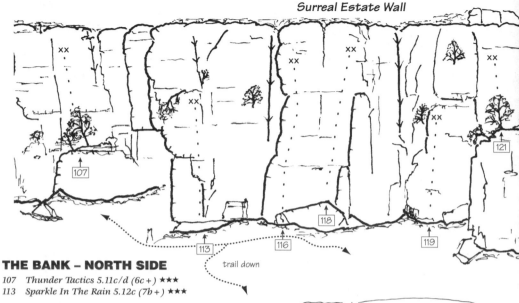

Surreal Estate Wall

trail down

THE BANK – NORTH SIDE

107   *Thunder Tactics 5.11c/d (6c+)* ★★★
113   *Sparkle In The Rain 5.12c (7b+)* ★★★

SURREAL ESTATE WALL

116   *Heavy Weather 5.12a/b (7a+)* ★★★
118   *Surreal Estate 5.12c (7b+)* ★★★
119   *Ice Cream Hangover 5.11b/c (6c)* ★★
121   *Deforestation 5.10d (6b)* ★
124   *Peter Pan 5.11b (6c)* ★

BACK TO THE FUTURE WALL

128   *Suede Head 5.12d (7c)* ★★★
130   *Future Fossil 5.12c (7b+)* ★★★
132   *Back To The Future 5.11b/c (6c)* ★★★
135   *BC 5.9+ (5+)* ★
137   *Mighty Mouse 5.10c (6a+)*

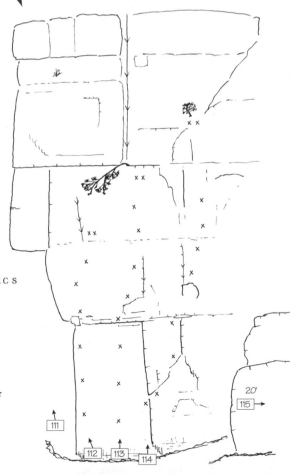

111   **Courage and Enlightenment** 5.11c s
      (6c)

112   **Staying Power** 5.11c (6c) ★★
      Balance, power.

113   **Sparkle In The Rain** 5.12c
      (7b+) ★★★
      Bulging, thin, sequential.

114   **Once Upon A Time** 5.11a (6b) ★★

20'

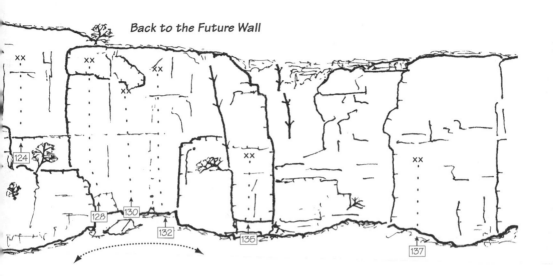

Back to the Future Wall

SURREAL ESTATE WALL

115 Stormy Weather 5.11a/b (6b+) ★
Face to roof.

116 Heavy Weather 5.12a/b (7a+) ★★★
Strenuous, devious.

117 Unusual Weather 5.11b/c (6c) ★★★
Continuous.

118 Surreal Estate 5.12c (7b+) ★★★
Technical, strenuous.

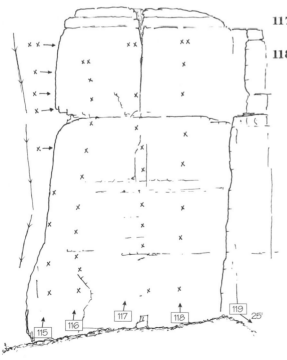

119 **Ice Cream Hangover** 5.11b/c (6c) ★★
Continuous, reaches.

120 **Le Pincher** 5.12d s (7c) ★
Very thin, tendon injury potential.

121 **Deforestation** 5.10d (6b) ★

122 **Moaner** 5.10c (6a+) ★

123 **5.9 Crack** 5.9 s (5)
Pro to 3".

124 **Peter Pan** 5.11b (6c) ★

125 **5.10 Crack** 5.10b s (6a)
Pro to 5".

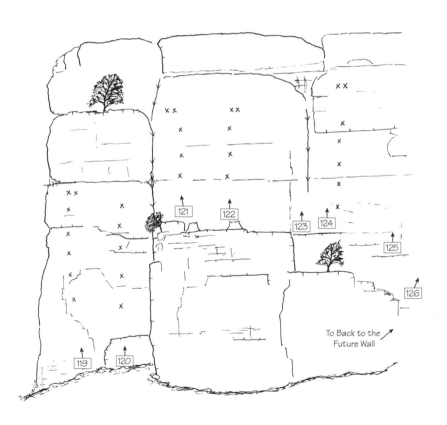

To Back to the
Future Wall

BACK TO THE FUTURE WALL

126 **Side Of Bacon** 5.11b/c (6c) ★★
Good position.

127 **This Is Your Brain** 5.12d (7c) ★★★
Thin, continuous.

128 **Suede Head** 5.12d (7c) ★★★
Very thin, continuous.

129 **No Rest For The Wicked** 5.12a (7a) ★★★
Very continuous, strenuous.

130 **Future Fossil** 5.12c (7b+) ★★★
Technical, continuous, strenuous.

131 **McFly** 5.12d (7c) ★★★
Thin, continuous.

132 **Back To The Future** 5.11b/c (6c) ★★★
Strenuous, power moves.

133 **No Future For The Timid** 5.11d (7a) ★★
Strenuous.

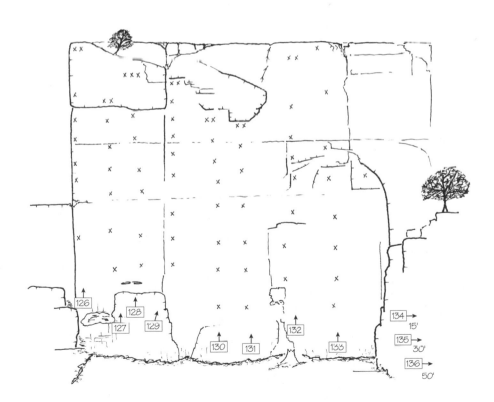

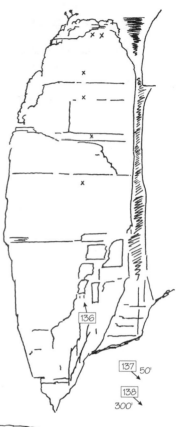

134   Rock Frog 5.10c/d (6b)

135   BC 5.9+ (5+) ★

136   Concentrated Weirdness 5.8+ (5) ★

137   Mighty Mouse 5.10c (6a+)

138   The Devil Made Me Dog It 5.12c (7b+) ★
Sharp.

139   The Lesser Of Two Evils 5.11b (6c) ★

140   Mismatched Partners 5.10b/c (6a)

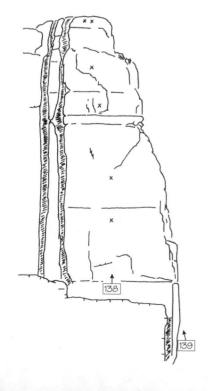

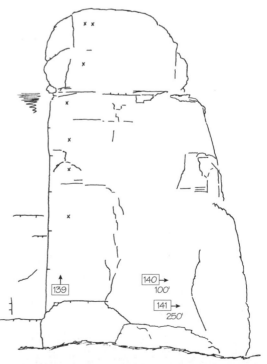

THE BANK – NORTH SIDE

143 *Aerial Solution 5.10c (6a+)*
144 *Tribal Boundary 5.11c (6c)* ★

2150 WALL

147 *Lime Street 5.11b (6c)* ★★★
152 *Taping Tendons 5.11c/d (6c+)* ★★★

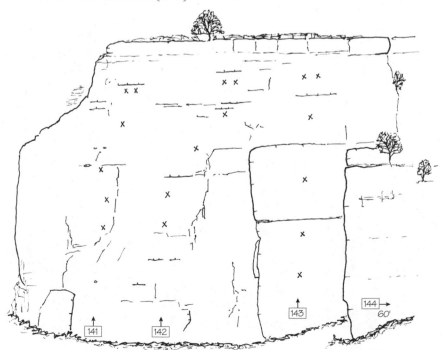

THE BANK–NORTH SIDE

139 The Lesser Of Two Evils 5.11b (6c) ★
140 Mismatched Partners 5.10b/c (6a)
142 Dancin' Shoes 5.10d (6b)
145 Primal Scream 5.9+ (5+) ★

141   Ethics? What Ethics? 5.11a/b (6b+)

142   Dancin' Shoes 5.10d (6b)

143   Aerial Solution 5.10c (6a+)

2150 WALL

147 Lime Street 5.11b (6c) ★★★
152 Taping Tendons 5.11c/d (6c+) ★★★
155 TB 5.11a (6b)

2150 Wall

trail down

300'
155 →

145

147

152

144   **Tribal Boundary** 5.11c (6c) ★
145   **Primal Scream** 5.9+ (5+) ★

145

144

146

40'

2150 WALL

146 Emperors Robe 5.11d (7a) ★★
Reaches.

147 Lime Street 5.11b (6c) ★★★,
Continuous, sharp, strenuous.

148 Aoxomoxoa 5.12b (7b) ★★
Thin, good protection.

149 Serious Power Outage 5.10c/d s (6b)

150 Ripped 5.10c (6a+)
Pro to 4".

151 Living in America 5.12a (7a) ★★★
Strenuous.

152 Taping Tendons 5.11c/d (6c+) ★★★
Continuous, sharp.

153 Lost Planet Airman 5.11c (6c) ★★★
Thin, continuous, sharp.

154 2150 A.D. 5.11a/b (6b+) ★★
Crack.

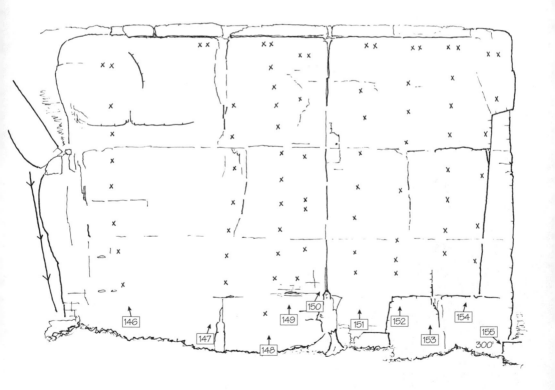

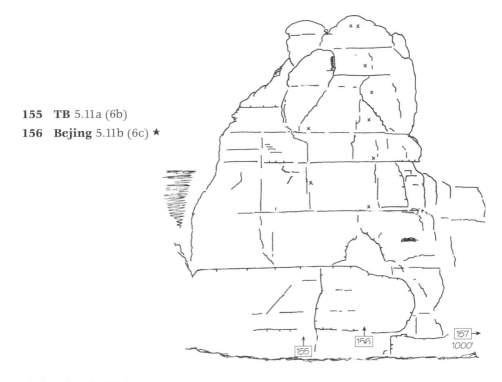

155 **TB** 5.11a (6b)

156 **Bejing** 5.11b (6c) ★

Mark Van Horn on Heavy Weather 5.12a/b (7a+). photo by Dan Monroe.

157 Pulling Down In The Fields Of Cotton 5.10c (6a+) ★
good rock

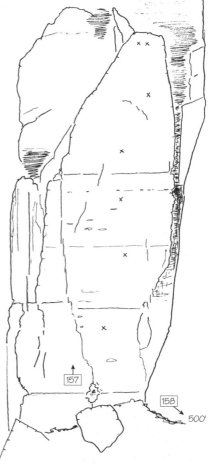

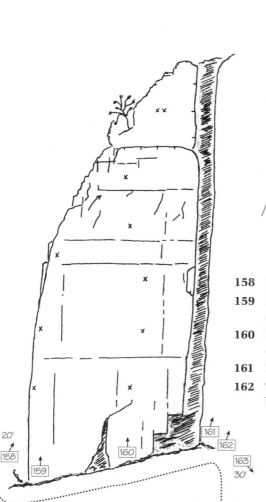

158 Enola Gay 5.8 (5) pro to 5.11 ★

159 Holiday In Cambodia 5.10c (6a+) ★
arete

160 Breakfast In Bhopal 5.11d (7a) ★
continuous

161 Handyman 5.8 (5) pro to 4"

162 Traditional Trickery 5.10b s (6a) 1
bolt/pro to 2.5"

163   **unknown** 5.12??

164   **Welcome To Shelf Road** 5.10d (6b) ★

165   **Sonic Youth** 5.11b/c (6c) ★

166   **unknown** 5.11b s (6c)

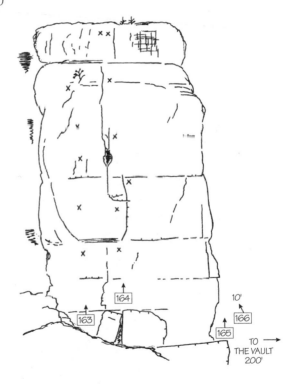

THE VAULT

The Vault is a small canyon which lies between The Bank and Cactus Cliff and hosts the Gem Wall (north facing) and The Cash Wall (south facing), both featuring a good selection of hard (5.12 and 5.13) routes. Assorted other east-facing routes are also found here.

To begin the approach for The Vault, park at the Bank Daypark area. From the parking area hike into The Bank several hundred feet to the 2150 Wall trailhead. Take this trail most of the way to the 2150 Wall, until another trail splits off to the right (east) at a sign that says "Gem Wall." This trail accesses The Vault area (as well as the eastern-most routes in The Bank). After traveling east through The Bank the cliff makes a distinct turn to the left (north) and Cactus Cliff becomes visible to the northeast. The Vault is encountered after approximately another 200 feet of hiking. Approach time; 15-20 min. (Future BLM plans will provide for a new parking area near Cactus Cliff; when completed, this will make the approach easier and shorter.)

THE VAULT

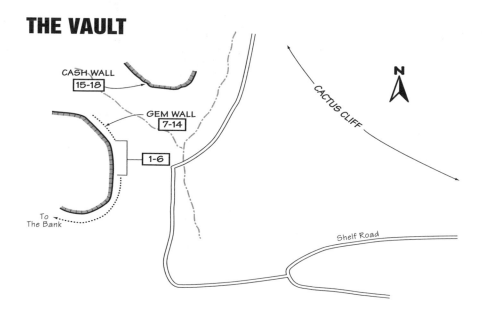

THE VAULT

1   **Pocket Change** 5.11c s (6c) ★

2   **Illusions** 5.11a/b s (6b +) ★★★
good position

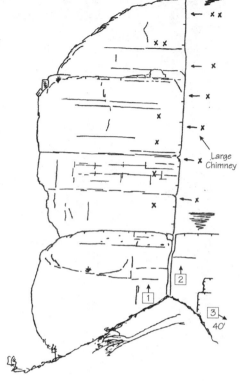

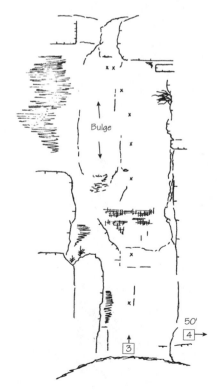

3   **Smoldering Horse Flesh** 5.11d
(7a) ★★
strenuous

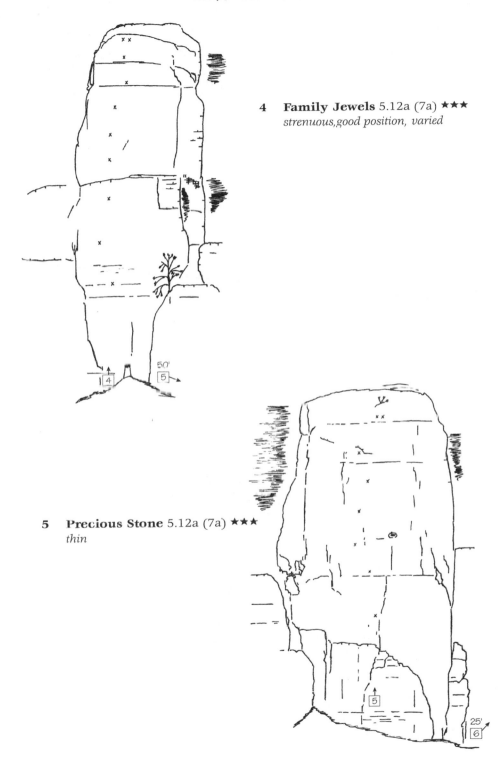

4   Family Jewels 5.12a (7a) ★★★
strenuous,good position, varied

5   Precious Stone 5.12a (7a) ★★★
thin

6   Easy Money 5.11a/b (6b+) ★

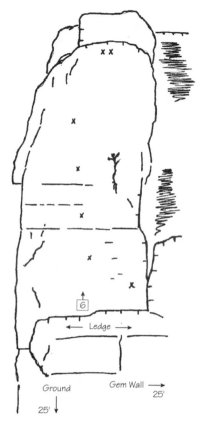

THE GEM WALL

7   14 Carats 5.12a/b (7a+) ★★★
thin, technical

8   What's The Combo 5.12a (7) ★★

9   unknown 5.12d/5.13a (7c)
very thin

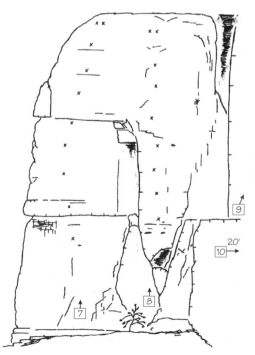

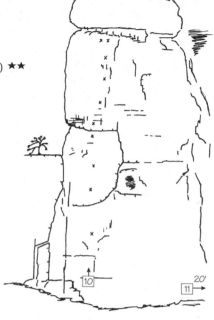

10   Jewel Of The Wild 5.12a (7a) ★★
good position

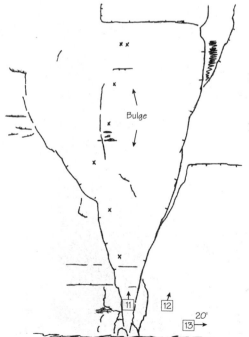

11   Splitting The Stone
5.11c/d (6c+) ★★
strenuous

12   Diamond In The Rough
5.12c/d (7c) ★★
tr-only

13 The Gem 5.12c (7b+) ★★★
continuous, strenuous

14 unknown 5.11b (6c) ★

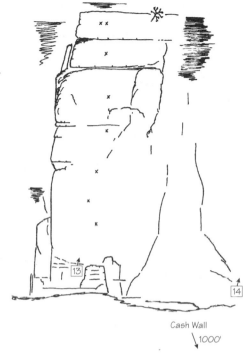

Cash Wall
↘ *1000'*

CASH WALL

15 Payment In Pump 5.13a/b (8a) ★★★
strenuous, great rock, gymnastic

16 Cache In The Vault 5.12d/5.13a (7c) ★★★
very thin, great rock

17 Money Changers 5.12b (7b) ★

18 Wad Of Dead Presidents 5.11c/d (6c+) ★

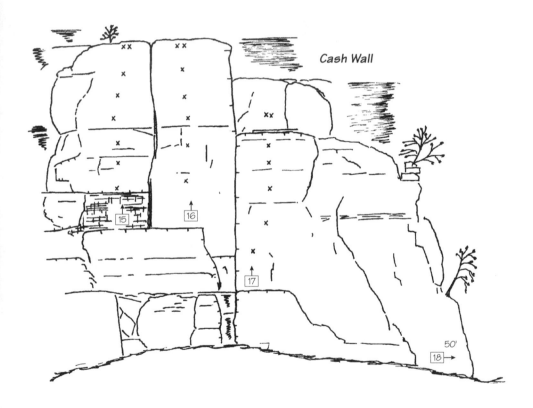

Cash Wall

Spiney Ridge

Cactus Cliff

Shelf Road

CACTUS CLIFF

Rising high above the Shelf Road lies one of the areas foremost cliffs, the Cactus Cliff. Multi-colored, first rate rock characterizes one of Shelfs' quintessential crags. It is easy to understand why this high profile cliff was one of the earliest crags ever explored. During a brief period of development during the 1980's, crack climbs kept pace with the sport climbs being established, a trend which has not occurred in the other areas of Shelf Road. After initial development, this crag was closed to rockclimbing by it's original land owner, however recent land status changes have been negotiated thanks to the efforts of The Access Fund and the BLM office in Canon City. The southern exposure of this cliff makes it an ideal winter crag.

Begin the approach to Cactus Cliff by parking at the Bank Daypark area. Follow the directions to the Vault. Continue through the Vault and cross through the drainage below the now obvious Cactus Cliff, which is visible to the northeast. Approach Time; 20-30 mins. (Future BLM plans will provide for a new parking area, near Cactus Cliff, making the approach easier and shorter.)

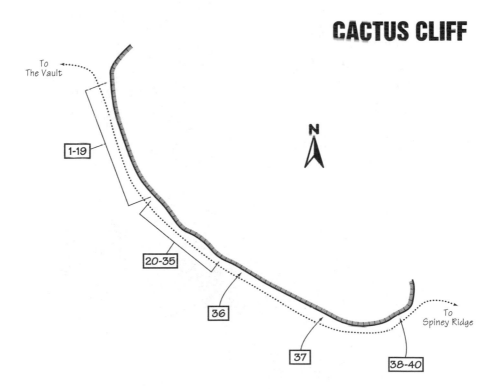

CACTUS CLIFF

To
The Vault

N

1-19

20-35

36

37

38-40

To
Spiney Ridge

Cactus Cliff/West

CACTUS CLIFF
West

1   Slicer 5.10d (6b) ★

2   Barbed Wire Love 5.10b (6a) ★

3   Crynoid Corner 5.7 (4) ★
pro to 4".

4   Hair Trigger 5.12c/d (7c) ★★★

5   Jumpin' The Gun 5.11d (7a) ★★★

6   Mark & Mark Route 5.11d or 5.12a (7a) ★
bolts/pro to 2".

Cactus Cliff

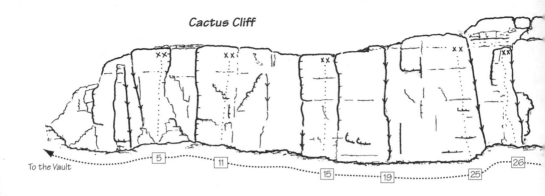

To the Vault

7   **Purple Corner** 5.7+ (4 s)
    pro to 4".

8   **unknown** 5.12?? ★★

9   **Illegal Smile** 5.11b (6c) s ★★

10 **unknown** 5.12?? ★★

11 **Fantasia** 5.11c (6c) ★★

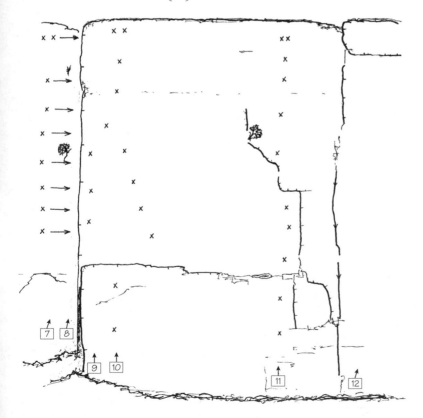

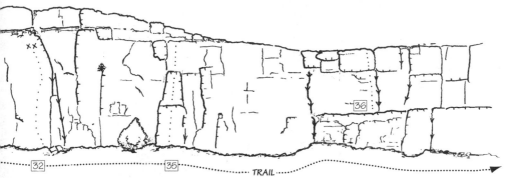

12   unknown 5.12?? ★★

13   Working Man 5.12b (7b) ★★

14   The Alignment 5.11a (6b) ★
   2 bolts/pro to 2".

15   unknown 5.13a (7c+) ★★★

16   Glue Slippage 5.12a (7a) ★★
   pro to 3".

17   The Killer Toupee 5.9+ (5+) s ★
   pro to 4".

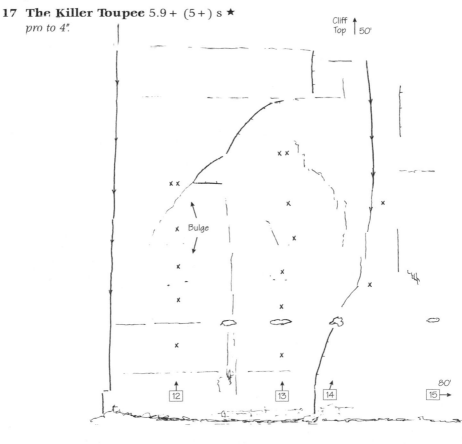

18 unknown 5.12? ★★★

19 Awesome Offwidthin' 5.10d (6b) ★★
pro to 6".

20 unknown 5.12?? ★★★

21 unknown 5.12a/b (7a+) ★★★

22 Glass Babies 5.9 (5) s ★★
pro to 2".

23 unknown 5.12b (7b) ★★★

24 Hot Bitch On A Beach 5.12b (7b) ★★★

25 Tits Up!! 5.12b (7b) ★★★

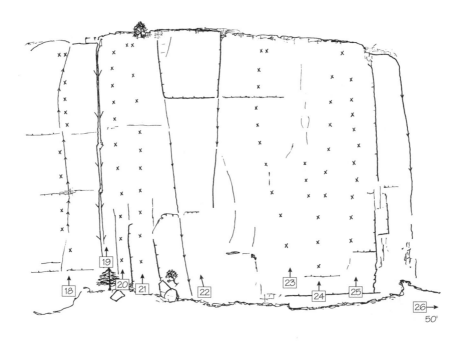

26 Third Stage 5.10a (5+) ★★★

27 Red Giant 5.9 (5) s ★★
pro to 4".

28 Lats Don't Have Feelings 5.11d (7a) ★★★

29 Under A Blood Red Wall 5.12a/b (7a+) ★★

30 Internal Dialog 5.11c (6c) ★
pro to 2"/1 bolt.

31 Gravitations 5.11d (7a) ★★★

32 The French Are Here 5.12c
(7b+) ★★★

33 The New Ethics 5.12b (7b) ★★

34 Corner To Roof 5.8 (5) ★
pro to 4".

35 Child Play 5.11d (7a) s ★
4 bolts

36 Bonkathon 5.11d/5.12a s (7a) ★
2 bolts/pro to 2".

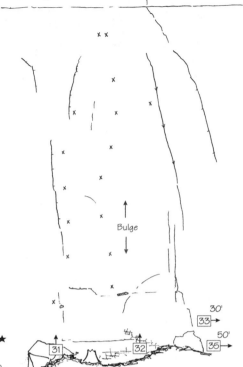

East

37 Almost French 5.11d/5.12a (7a) ★★

38 project 5.11? ★★
1 bolt

39 I Quesada 5.10b/c s (6a) ★★
pro to 4".

40 Ain't Noth'n' But A Hangdog 5.12a (7a) ★★

41 I Claudius 5.11b s (6c) ★★
pro to 2".

Unlisted cracks Locations unknown

Leapiní Lizards 5.8 (5)
pro to 4".

Little Bald Men 5.8+(5)
pro to 4".

Solar Flare 5.10c (6a+)
pro to 2".

Wasp Tower 5.8 (5) vs
pro to 3".

Fred 5.9/5
pro to 3".

The Wedge 5.9/5
pro to 3".

Cactus Cliff/East

Spiney Ridge

SPINEY RIDGE

Spiney Ridge is a small buttress of cliffband overlooking the valley in scenic Helena Canyon. The view of the valley includes the Sangre de Cristo range in the vast background, certainly one of Colorado's most beautiful sights. Like it's neighbor to the west (Cactus Cliff), Spiney Ridge offers plenty of sunshine and warm winter cragging.

To approach Spiney Ridge, begin by parking at the Bank Daypark area. Follow the directions to Cactus Cliff, then continue east along the cliffband, passing a prominent gully which separates Spiney Ridge form Cactus Cliff. (Future BLM plans will provide for a new parking area, near Cactus Cliff, making the approach easier and shorter.)

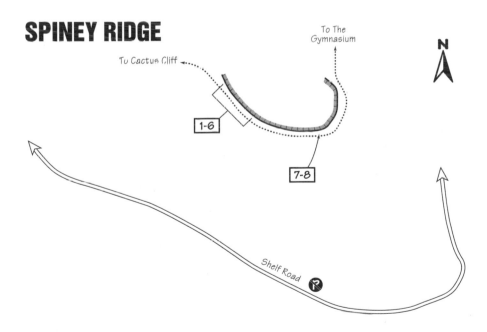

SPINEY RIDGE

To The Gymnasium

To Cactus Cliff

N

1-6

7-8

Shelf Road

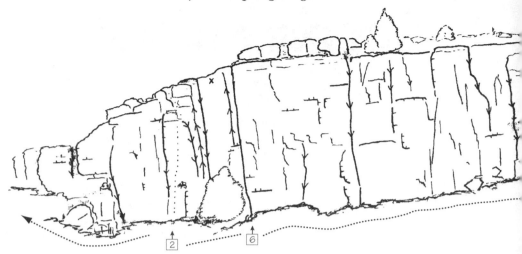

SPINEY RIDGE

1 **Cheers** 5.8+ s (5)
pro to 3".

2 **Tractatus** 5.11a (6b)

3 **Sunday Pockets** 5.10a s (9+)
pro to 3".

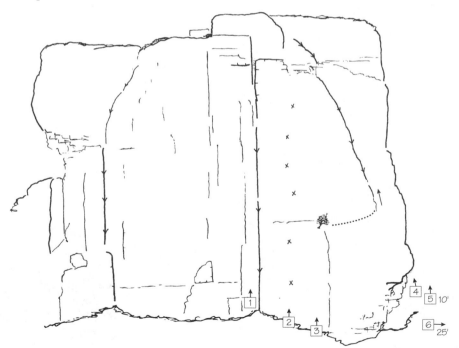

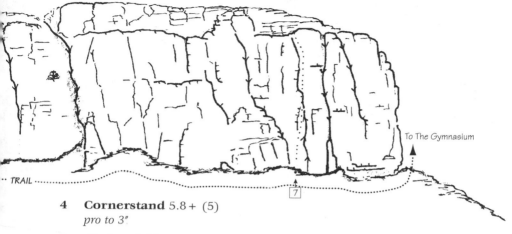

4   **Cornerstand** 5.8 + (5)
pro to 3"

5   **project** 5.12

6   **2oth Century Man** 5.9 + (5 +)
pro to 3"

7   **Cornerstone** 5.10c/d s (6b)
3 bolts/pro to 2"

8   **unknown** 5.10c/d s (6b)
pro to 4"

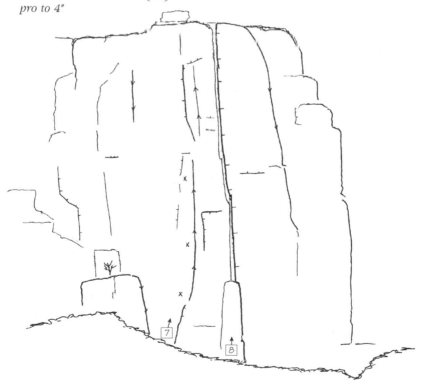

THE GYMNASIUM

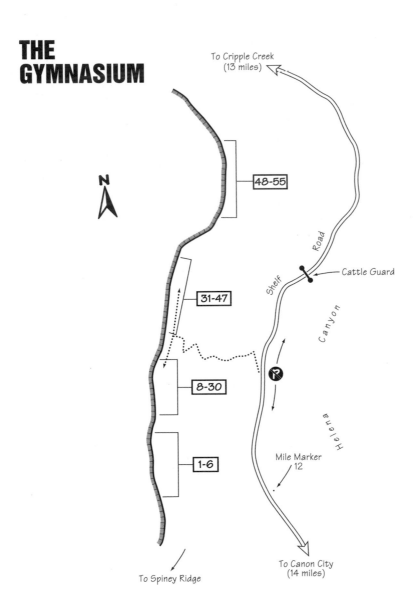

To Cripple Creek
(13 miles)

N

48-55

Shelf Road

Cattle Guard

Canyon

31-47

8-30

Helena

1-6

Mile Marker
12

To Spiney Ridge

To Canon City
(14 miles)

THE GYMNASIUM

With scenic views, high cliffs, and quality limestone, The Gymnasium is a premier rock climbing crag. Situated high above Shelf Road in Helena Canyon, this extensive, east-facing wall offers some of Shelf Road's best and most difficult routes.

A good trail leaves Shelf Road 0.25 mile past the 12-mile marker. The trail switchbacks left (west) up the steep hillside. Approach time varies from 10 to 60 minutes, depending on your parking strategy. Note that Shelf Road is closed to unattended vehicles between mile markers 10 and 14.

BANK-DARK SIDE-CACTUS CLIFF-SPINEY RIDGE-GYMNASIUM
OVERVIEW

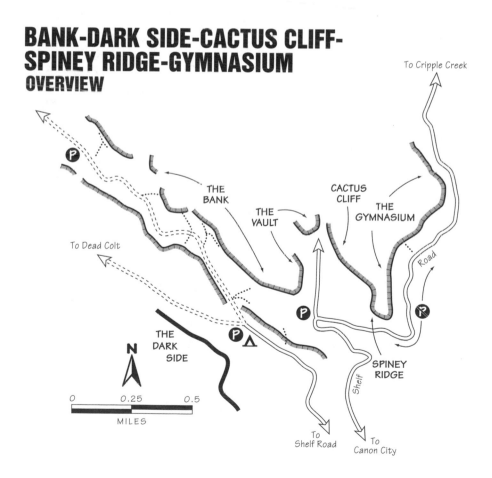

THE GYMNASIUM OVERVIEW

1   Natty Dread 5.11c/6c
very continuous

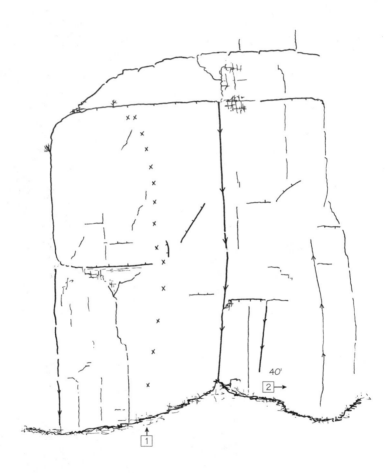

2 **Fat Burger** 5.13a/b/8a
technical

3 **unknown** 5.12c/7b +
thin

4 **New Rule** 5.9 + /5 +
good rock, thin

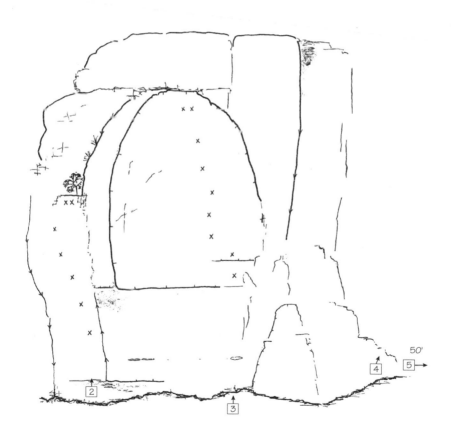

5   Untapped 5.12c/7b +
very continuous

6   Our Bosch Of The Immaculate Conception 5.10d s/6b

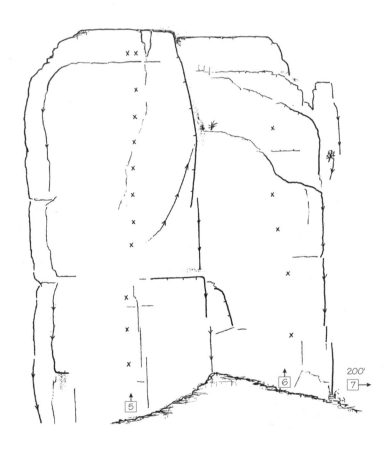

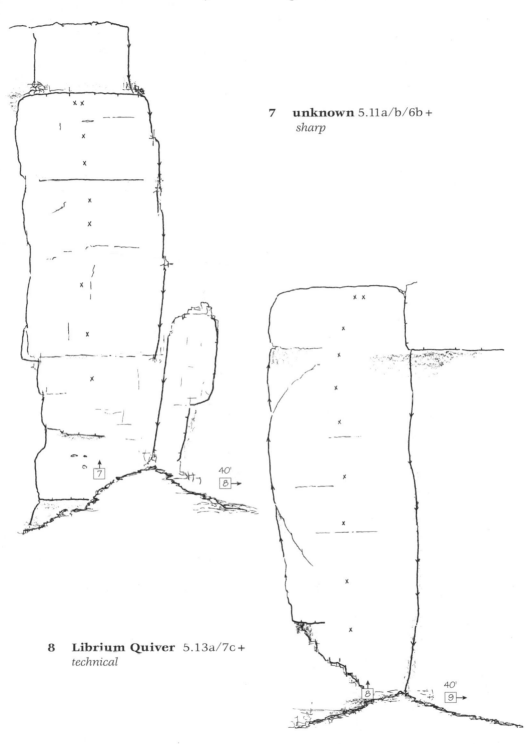

7 unknown 5.11a/b/6b+
sharp

8 Librium Quiver 5.13a/7c+
technical

9   unknown 5.12d/7c
very continuous

10   Butt Flambe' 5.11c/d/6c+
continuous

11   Here Today, Gone Tomorrow 5.12b/7b
good position

12   Paradise Regained 5.12c/7b+
continuous

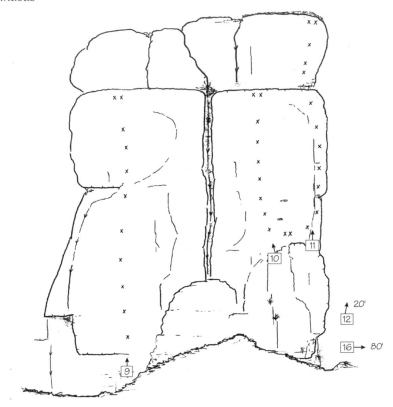

13 unknown 5.12c/7b+

14 Spontaneous Combustion 5.12a/7a

15 unknown 5.11b/c/6c

16 I Never Met A Carbo I Didn't Like 5.11d/7a
good rock

17 I Am A Machine 5.11d/7a
good rock, pockets

18 Pinhead 5.10a/b/6a
good rock

19 Scarface 5.12a/7a

20 VHS or BETA 5.11c/d/6c+
good rock, technical

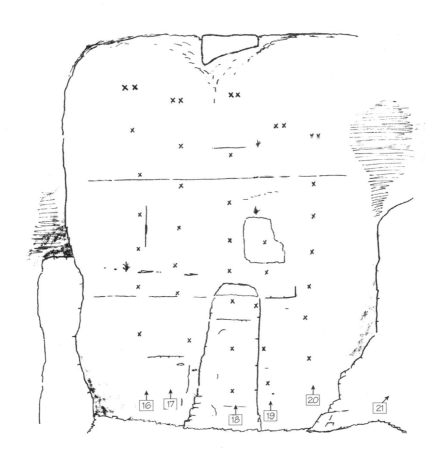

21 **The Ejection Seat** 5.12b/c/7b
power moves, sequential

22 **The Ejection Generation** 5.12c/7b+
contiuous

23 **My Generation** 5.13a/7c+
continuous, technical

24 **Bottom Feeder** 5.13a/7c+
continuous, technical

(project) 5.??

(project) 5.??

25 **Crystal** 5.11b/6c
good rock, thin

26 **The Great Escape** 5.11c/6c
good rock, thin

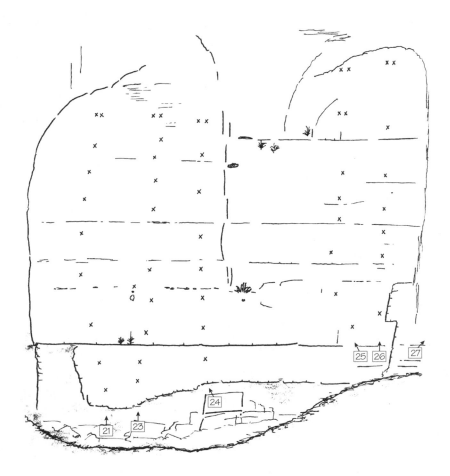

27 Morning Stretch 5.11b/6c
power moves

28 It's OK To Fart 5.12b/c/7b

29 No Shelf Control 5.12c/d/7c

30 Bubba's Belly 5.12c/7b+
thin, bulging

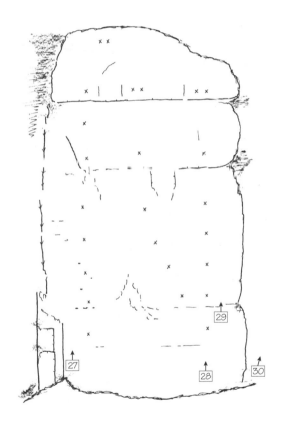

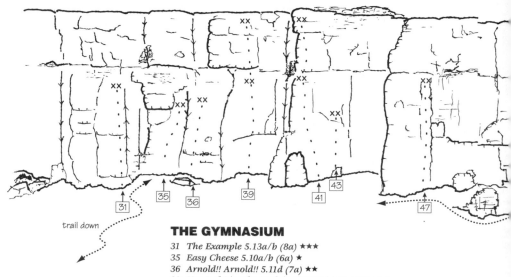

trail down

THE GYMNASIUM

31 *The Example 5.13a/b (8a)* ★★★
35 *Easy Cheese 5.10a/b (6a)* ★
36 *Arnold!! Arnold!! 5.11d (7a)* ★★
39 *Hot Rod Lincoln 5.11b/c & 5.12c/d (6c & 7c)* ★★
41 *Cimmaron Lanes 5.11d &5.10d (7a & 6b)* ★★★
43 *Jane Fonda's Warm-up 5.11a (6b)* ★
47 *Needle Haven 5.10b (6a)* ★
48 *Deeper Shade Of Soul 5.13b (8a)* ★★★
52 *Earth Moves 5.11c (6c)* ★★
55 *Bone n' Vein 5.12c (7b +)* ★★

THE GYMNASIUM

31 The Example 5.13a/b (8a) ★★★
Great rock, continuous, technical.

32 The Gym Arête 5.12c/d & 5.12b
(7c & 7b) ★★★
Great rock, continuous, technical.

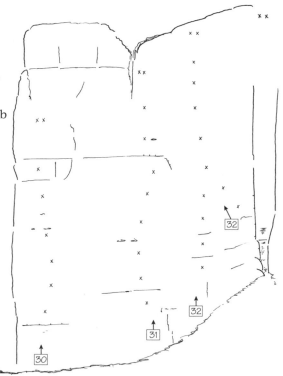

33 The Crack of Dawn 5.10b (6a) ★★

34 Head Cheese 5.12c/d (7c) ★★
Technical, roofs.

35 Easy Cheese 5.10a/b (6a) ★

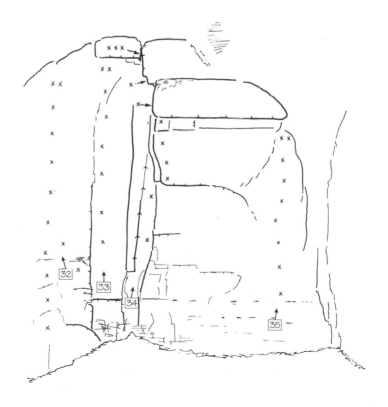

36 Arnold!! Arnold!! 5.11d (7a) ★★
Power moves.

37 Solar Flex 5.11c (6c) ★

38 Five Dollars 5.10c (6a+) ★

39 Hot Rod Lincoln 5.11b/c & 5.12c/d (6c & 7c) ★★
Two pitches; thin, technical.

40 Com'in In Smooth 5.11b/c (6c) ★★
Good rock, thin, technical.

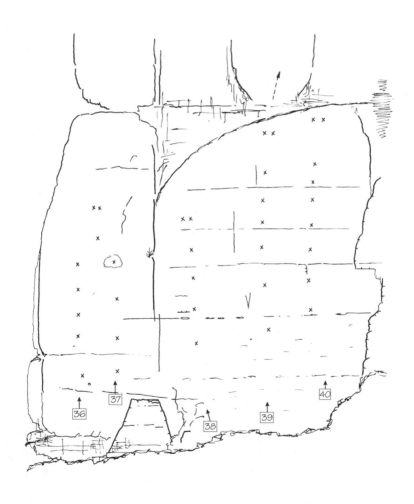

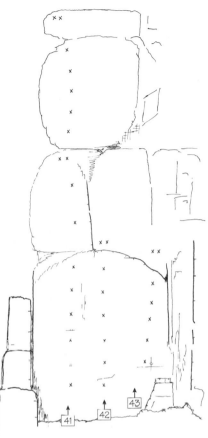

41 Cimmaron Lanes 5.11d &5.10d
(7a & 6b) ★★★
Two pitches; very continuous.

42 Orange Marmalade 5.12a (7a) ★

43 Jane Fonda's Warmup 5.11a
(6b) ★

44 Pump Up And Air Out 5.12b/c
(7b) ★★
Thin, technical.

45 Unknown 5.12a (7a)

46 Unknown 5.11c (6c) ★

47 Needle Haven 5.10b (6a) ★
Rockfall between Routes 47 and 48.

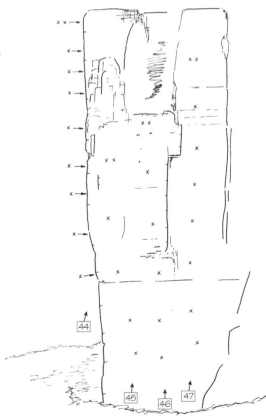

48 Deeper Shade Of Soul 5.13b (8a) ★★★
Good position, very thin.

49 Bone Daddy 5.12d (7c) ★★
Thin.

50 Hammer Therapy 5.12c (7b+) ★

51 Project 5.13a (7c+) ★★

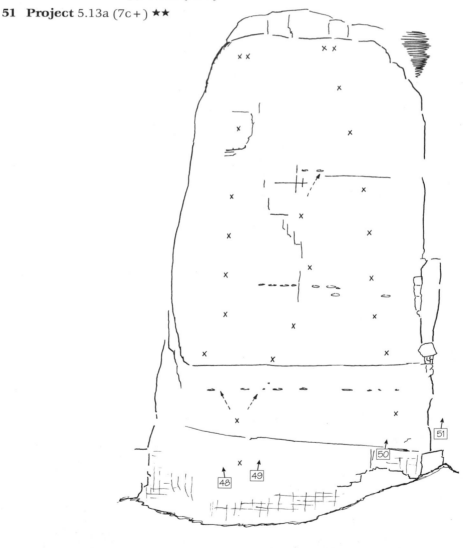

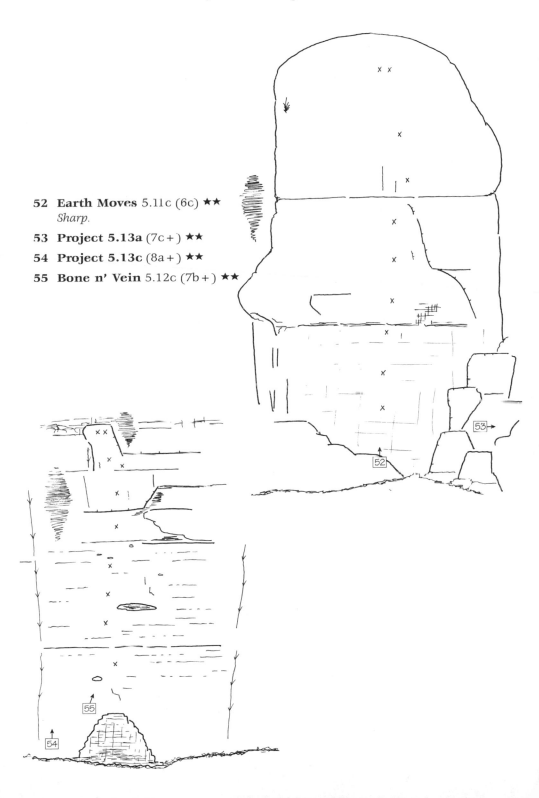

52 Earth Moves 5.11c (6c) ★★
Sharp.

53 Project 5.13a (7c+) ★★

54 Project 5.13c (8a+) ★★

55 Bone n' Vein 5.12c (7b+) ★★

APPENDIX A

Route quality assessed on a scale of one to four stars. No stars equates to a pile while four stars designates a mega classic.

SAND GULCH
Contest Wall

*Cumulocrimpus 12a ***

Guess what the forecast for this route will be. The first route on the Contest Wall. Start eight feet left of Vail Athletic Club and follow six bolts through a bulge to a pair of Fixé rap anchors. 45 feet. FA: Rick Thompson & Pat Thompson, May 1997.

*Regroovable 11b ****

A fine combination of pockets and edges! Start immediately right of *Cactus Drop* and follow seven camouflaged bolts to a pair of Fixé rap anchors. 60 feet. FA: Rick Thompson & Pat Thompson, April 1998.

*Pocket Laurearête 12a *****

Trick name, trick pockets—short n' sweet! Locate the ledge around the corner and 50 feet left of *You Snooze, You Lose*. Climb the narrow panel of perfect rock protected by five bolts to a pair of Fixé rap anchors. The bolts are well camoíed, so you may have to look closely to locate this route. 40 feet. FA: Rick Thompson & Pat Thompson, April 1998.

*Sprayburn 12a/b ***

Inspired by Speyburn, a tasty Speyside single malt scotch. Begin ten feet left of *Primal Urge* and follow the offset, tiny corner to a bulge. Fire past the business and finesse the clean face to a pair of rap anchors. Eight bolts in all. 60 feet. FA: Rick Thompson & Kevin Vowels, March 1998.

SAND GULCH
Freeform Wall

*The Pedestrian Gene Pool 11b ***

A slightly contrived stroll through the rock garden. The original line followed holds just right of the third and fourth bolts then crossed leftward at the fifth bolt. However, most pedestrians prefer straying further right on bigger holds until well past the fifth bolt ñ the difficulty for this version is slightly easier. Begin between *Cyborg and Partners in Crime* and climb the short flake to a ledge and follow bolts to a pair of rap anchors. Seven bolts. 50 feet. FA: Rick Thompson, Pat Thompson & Azenda Cater, January 1998.

THE GALLERY
Mural Wall

*Magnum Groups 11c ***

Thin start to a gropey crux. Begin ten feet left of *Morpheus* (and follow six bolts to a pair of Fixé rap anchors. 50 feet. FA: Pat Thompson, Rick Thompson & Azenda Cater, January 1998.

*Morpheus 11b ***

The Greek god of dreams. Nice pockets and a pair of juggy roofs—has become a popular warm-up for the Mural Wall classics. Begin ten feet left of *M&M* and follow seven bolts to a pair of FixÈ rap anchors. 55 feet. FA: Rick Thompson & Pat Thompson, January 1998.

*Pretty Fastidium 12a ***

A mood of scornful distaste. Start midway between the Mural Wall and *Block Party* at a short left-facing corner in reddish rock and follow seven bolts up the gently overhanging face and over a small roof to a pair of Fixé rap anchors. 50 feet. FA: Jeff Bates, Mike Shelton, & Rick Thompson, February 1998.

*Block Party 10b ***

Left of *Morrocan Roll* is a left-facing dihedral. Begin about ten feet left of the dihedral and climb the slabby face past two bolts to the top of the detached pillar. Continue directly up the gently overhanging face past four more bolts to a pair of Fixé rap anchors. 55 feet. FA: Jeff Bates & Rick Thompson, January 1998.

Morrocan Roll—updated gear—the runout start is now protected by three additional bolts compliments of Bob Robertson.

THE GALLERY
Menses Prow

Weed 'n Feed 10b

Right of *No Passion for Fashion* is a right-facing dihedral. Begin ten feet to the right and follow the bolted crack to a pair of anchors. 50 feet. FA: Bob & Carry Robertson, December 1997.

A Sheep in Wolf's Clothing 12a/b *

A deceptive limestone lamb. Despite the cheesy start, you'll encounter good climbing and great position. Begin ten feet right of *General #4* (the most right hand of the four Kurt Smith routes) with a stick clip, and crank past the "rock-atto" (as in cheese) start, then follow six more bolts through a burly roof to a pair of Fixé rap anchors. 50 feet. FA: Rick Thompson, January 1998.

THE DARK SIDE
Red Devil 11b *

Yikes . . . is that a limestone fist crack? You betcha! Commence 12 feet right of *The Eagle Has Landed* and follow the varying width crack to a demonic arete finish with more bolts than you clip. 10 bolts. 75 feet. FA: Pat Thompson, October 1998.

Fat Like Butta 11d *

An apt description of the pockets on the first half of the route, but things thin out for the finish. Begin from a ledge eight feet right of *The Eagle Has Landed*, just left of the crack start of Red Devil, and follow 10 bolts to a pair of Fixé rap anchors. 80 feet. FA: Rick Thompson, October 1998.

Animatronic 11b ***

A variety pack of continuous and technical climbing makes this one a new-veau Shelf classic. Start immediately right of *The Audition* and follow nine camo'd bolts to a pair of Fixé rap anchors. 80 feet. FA: Rick Thompson, Pat Thompson, & Jana Elliott, June 1998.

Porkus Procurement 10d *

For a taste of the "other white meat" start just left of *Enchanted Porkfist* and balance up and left on a stepped-ramp until it peters out, then wallow directly up the sustained face to a pair of Metolius rap anchors. Six bolts in all. 55 feet. FA: Rick Thompson, Pat Thompson, & Jana Elliott, June 1998.

APPENDIX B

Bureau Of Land Management (BLM)
3170 East Main Street (U.S. Highway 50)
Canon City, Colorado 81212
719-269-8500

Mountain Chalet
226 N. Tejon Street
Colorado Springs, CO 80903
719-633-0732

Rocky Mountain Field Institute
1520 Alamo Avenue
Colorado Springs, CO 80907
719-471-7736

The Sport Climbing Center
4650 Northpark Dr.
Colorado Springs, CO 80918
(719)-260-1050

Nearest hospital/emergency room

Centura Health/Thomas Moore Hospital
1338 Phay Avenue
Canon City, CO 81212
719-269-2000

INDEX

ACCESS FUND OPENS MORE SHELF ROAD CRAGS

by Rick Thompson

The second in a string of nationally significant Access Fund land acquisitions is poised for completion in May, 1999. The Access Fund has agreed to purchase 115 acres that include 1.5 miles of high quality cliff-line. Included will be The Vault, Gem Wall, Cash Wall, Cactus Cliff, Spiney Ridge, the southern half of The Gym, and a portion of The North End in the vicinity of Heaven. The acquisition has been carefully coordinated with the BLM, which will subsequently purchase the property from the Access Fund and provide for the area's long-term management. Together, the Fund and the BLM will invest more than $125,000 in opening the area. This acquisition will consolidate BLM ownership in the area, essentially reducing the routes on private property to less than 10 percent of the total.

Improvements associated with this acquisition will include a day parking area adjacent to the Cactus Cliff to provide efficient access to the nearby crags. In addition, a trail network for the newly opened cliffs will be designed in spring '99. Trail construction will be undertaken in fall '99, primarily with the help of volunteers, so stay tuned for details about this project, and check the Access Fund website for upcoming information on how you can volunteeer. The Rocky Mountain Field Institute (formerly the American Mountain Foundation), based in nearby Colorado Springs, will assist with the trail work. The majority of Shelf's outstanding trails have been constructed under the Field Institute's oversight during the past decade. Climbers owe thanks to both the Field Institute and the BLM for turning Shelf Road into the climbing mecca it is today.

Land acquisitions are just one of many ways the Access Fund is keeping you climbing. But we need your help to continue our critical work across the country - your membership. Join the Access Fund today by logging on to our website at www.accessfund.org, or call 303-545-6772 for more information. If you have questions about our land acquisitions program call Acquisitions Director Rick Thompson at 303.545.6772, ext. 105.

WE NEED YOUR SUPPORT TO PRESERVE FUTURE CLIMBING AT SHELF ROAD

Over the past decade miles of beautiful trails, day parking sites and campgrounds close to the crags have been built for the sole benefit of climbers, and at a cost to the BLM approaching $200,000. There are few climbing areas in the country that offer such an enjoyable, pro-climbing environment. To-date climbing at Shelf Road has remained cost free with one minor exception - an overnight camping fee. Sadly, the track record of climbers who pay this nominal fee is embarrasing - less than 30% have complied over the past few years. In 1998 the total camping fee receipts were less than $3,000 - not even enough to cover basic maintenance costs for the campsites you enjoy. PLEASE do your part to insure climbing here remains a welcome use - PAY YOUR CAMPING FEE UPON OCUPPYING YOUR SITE. Thanks!

ACCESS: It's every climber's concern

The Access Fund, a national, non-profit climbers organization, works to keep climbing areas open and to conserve the climbing environment. Need help with closures? land acquisition? legal or land management issues? funding for trails and other projects? starting a local climbers' group? CALL US! Climbers can help preserve access by being committed to Leave No Trace (minimum-impact) practices. Here are some simple guidelines:

• **ASPIRE TO "LEAVE NO TRACE"** especially in environmentally sensitive areas like caves. Chalk can be a significant impact on dark and porous rock—don't use it around historic rock art. Pick up litter, and leave trees and plants intact.

• **DISPOSE OF HUMAN WASTE PROPERLY** Use toilets whenever possible. If toilets are not available, dig a "cat hole" at least six inches deep and 200 feet from any water, trails, campsites, or the base of climbs. *Always pack out toilet paper.* On big wall routes, use a "poop tube" and carry waste up and off with you (the old "bag toss" is now illegal in many areas).

• **USE EXISTING TRAILS** Cutting switchbacks causes erosion. When walking off-trail, tread lightly, especially in the desert where cryptogamic soils (usually a dark crust) take thousands of years to form and are easily damaged. Be aware that "rim ecologies" (the clifftop) are often highly sensitive to disturbance.

• **BE DISCRETE WITH FIXED ANCHORS** *Bolts are controversial and are not a convenience* – don't place 'em unless they are *really* necessary. Camouflage all anchors. Remove unsightly slings from rappel stations (better to use steel chain or welded cold shuts). Bolts sometimes can be used proactively to protect fragile resources – consult with your local land manager.

• **RESPECT THE RULES** and speak up when other climbers don't. Expect restrictions in designated wilderness areas, rock art sites, caves, and to protect wildlife, especially nesting birds of prey. *Power drills are illegal in wilderness and all national parks.*

• **PARK AND CAMP IN DESIGNATED AREAS** Some climbing areas require a permit for overnight camping.

• **MAINTAIN A LOW PROFILE** Leave the boom box and day-glo clothing at home—the less climbers are heard and seen, the better.

• **RESPECT PRIVATE PROPERTY** Be courteous to land owners. Don't climb where you're not wanted.

• **JOIN THE ACCESS FUND!** To become a member, make a tax-deductible donation of $25 or more.

The Access Fund

Preserving America's Diverse Climbing Resources
PO Box 17010 Boulder, CO 80308
303.545.6772 • www.accessfund.org